Skills Practice
Workbook

**Level 2
Book 1**

Columbus, OH

SRAonline.com

 SRA

Send all inquiries to this address:
SRA/McGraw-Hill
4400 Easton Commons
Columbus, OH 43219-6188

ISBN: 978-0-07-610476-5
MHID: 0-07-610476-1

1 2 3 4 5 6 7 8 9 QPD 13 12 11 10 09 08 07

The *McGraw-Hill* Companies

① Kindness

Unit 2 Let's Explore

(3) Around the Town

Unit 3

Name _Caldic Pals_ Date _2-7-20_

/ā/ Sound and Spellings

 (-1) 92%

Focus • The /ā/ sound can be spelled with *a* and *a__e*.

Practice Read the following words. Underline the *a* or *a__e* spelling pattern used in each word.

1. b<u>a</u>sic   5. c<u>a</u>n<u>e</u>

2. r<u>a</u>k<u>e</u>   6. h<u>a</u>lo

3. f<u>a</u>d<u>e</u>   7. <u>a</u>bl<u>e</u>

4. navy   8. b<u>a</u>sis

Replace the underlined letter or letters with the given letter to create a rhyming word. The new word will have the same spelling for the /ā/ sound. Write the word on the line.

1. <u>f</u> able + t = _table_

2. <u>w</u> ave + g = _gave_

3. <u>l</u> ace + f = _face_

4. <u>m</u> ade + f = _fade_

5. <u>c</u> able + st = _stable_

Apply **Choose a word from the box below to complete each sentence. Write the word on the line.**

| bacon | taste | bakes | trade | table | apron |

1. My favorite breakfast is eggs and _____.

2. I will _____ you my apple for your banana.

3. Could you please set the _____ for dinner?

4. Aunt Lucy _____ the best cookies.

5. Dad wears mom's _____ when he is cooking.

6. Kathy can't wait to _____ the pie.

Circle the correct spelling of each word.

1.   baceon   bacon

2.   fak   fake

3.   daet   date

4.   laezy   lazy

5.   naem   name

6.   raek   rake

Name _____ Date _____

/ī/ Sound and Spellings

Focus
- The /ī/ sound can be spelled with *i* or *i__e*.

Practice Read the following words out loud. Underline the *i* or *i__e* spelling pattern used in each word.

1. i d o l

2. r i d e

3. i t e m

4. p i p e

5. s i d e

6. p i l o t

7. h i k e

8. i r i s

Circle the words from above in the word search.

```
T  R  H  L  V  B  S  Z
I  I  D  O  P  I  P  E
U  D  M  I  I  T  E  A
W  E  O  C  L  X  H  E
A  Y  N  L  O  P  I  Z
I  Z  H  J  T  G  K  R
T  I  B  S  I  D  E  U
E  W  V  F  U  O  U  J
M  A  I  R  I  S  H  E
```

Apply Choose a word from the box below to complete each sentence. Write the word on the line.

iron	time	dime	virus	kite	idea

1. What _____ does school start?

2. A _____ is worth ten cents.

3. A _____ is making Kate feel sick.

4. I love to fly a _____ on windy days.

5. It was my _____ to eat ice cream for dessert.

6. My mom still needs to _____ my dress.

Circle the correct spelling of each word.

1.   ida   idea

2.   fir   fire

3.   wise   wis

4.   ireon   iron

5.   side   sid

6.   rise   ris

Name _____ Date _____

Selection Vocabulary

Focus

care *v.* To look after.

precious *adj.* Loved and cherished.

share *v.* To divide into portions and give to others as well as oneself.

feelings *n.* Plural of **feeling:** an emotion, such as joy, fear, or sadness.

kind *adj.* Gentle, giving, and friendly.

Practice Draw a line to match each word on the left to its definition on the right.

1. care

2. feelings

3. kind

4. precious

5. share

a. loved and cherished

b. to divide into portions and give to others as well as oneself

c. to look after

d. an emotion such as joy, fear, or sadness

e. gentle, generous, and friendly

Write a sentence using one or more vocabulary words.

_____

Apply **Use your understanding of the vocabulary words to complete the following activities.**

1. Write about a time you were able to *share* something.

2. List three examples of different *feelings.*

3. What is something that is *precious* to you?

4. Make a list of the people that take *care* of you?

5. Write one way you can be *kind* to someone else?

Name _____ Date _____

Recording Information

Pay close attention to how people act toward each other every day. Record acts of kindness and courtesy that you see.

Where did it happen?	Why did it happen?	Kindness or Courtesy	How did the person react?
1.			
2.			
3.			
4.			
5.			

How can you investigate kindness? You may have already started asking questions, such as what are examples of kindness. What else can you ask?

1. _____

2. _____

3. _____

As you begin exploring kindness, keep a list of things you need to do. Check off each item as you finish it. Here is a start. Add to it as you read the unit.

☐ Talk to friends about what being kind means.

☐ Talk to adults about kindness.

☐ Find and read books or stories about people or characters that show kindness.

Name _____ Date _____

Brainstorming Ideas

Acts of kindness can happen anywhere. Brainstorm ideas for places where you could do specific things to show kindness.

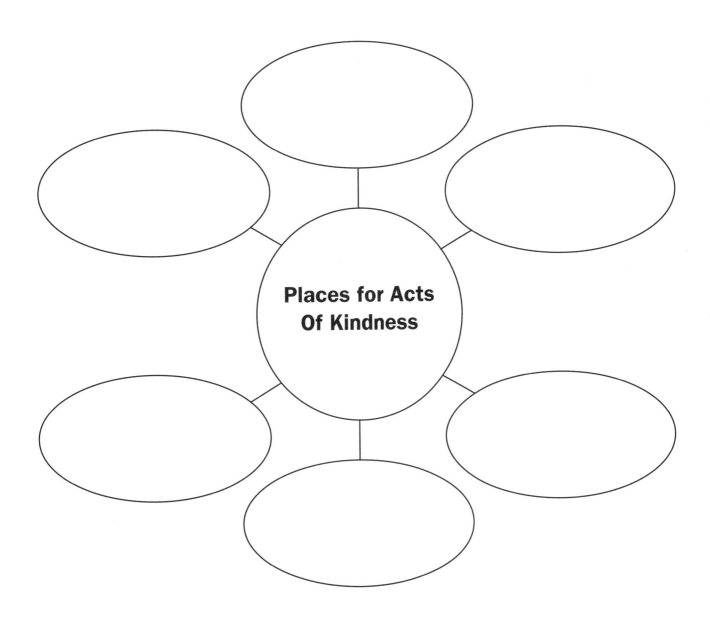

Places for Acts Of Kindness

Writing a List

Think **Audience: Who** will read your list?

_____

Purpose: What is your reason for writing a list?

_____

Prewriting **Choose one of the locations from your brainstorming graphic organizer. Make a list of possible kind things you could do at the location you choose.**

Title

Write acts of kindness you could do at this place.

1. _____

2. _____

3. _____

4. _____

5. _____

6. _____

Name _____   Date _____

Long Vowel a spelled *a* and *a_e*
Long Vowel i spelled *i* and *i_e*

Focus

- Long vowels sound like their names.
- Two ways long *a* can be spelled are *a* and *a_e*.
- Two ways long *i* can be spelled are *i* and *i_e*.

Word List

1. mild
2. care
3. pilot
4. lady
5. bake
6. time
7. sale
8. ride
9. able
10. kind

Challenge Words

11. apron
12. final
13. quite
14. quiet
15. share

Practice **Sort the spelling words under the correct heading.**

long a spelled *a*

1. _____
2. _____

long a spelled *a_e*

3. _____
4. _____
5. _____

long i spelled *i*

6. _____
7. _____
8. _____

long i spelled *i_e*

9. _____
10. _____

Apply **Rhyming Strategy** Write the spelling word that rhymes with each set of words below. The new word should have the same spelling pattern.

16. stare bare _____

17. cake make _____

18. side hide _____

19. cable table _____

20. wild child _____

Visualization Strategy Circle the correct spelling for each spelling word. Write the correct spelling on the line.

21. pilot pylet _____

22. lade lady _____

23. kinde kind _____

24. sael sale _____

25. time tiem _____

Name _____ Date _____

Alphabetical Order

Focus

- When words start with different letters, use the letter of each word to put the words in alphabetical order.

- When words start with the same first letter, use the next letter that is different in each word to put the words in alphabetical order.

Practice Put these words from the story "Because of You" in alphabetical order. Write the words on the lines.

can	of	and

_____   _____

_____   _____

_____   _____

Put these words from the story in alphabetical order.

child	countries	care

_____   _____   _____

Apply Put these words from the story in alphabetical order. Write the words on the lines.

world	peace	teach	precious	kind	help

1. _____   4. _____

2. _____   5. _____

3. _____   6. _____

Write three words of your own. Then write them again in alphabetical order.

_____   _____

_____   _____

_____   _____

Name _____ Date _____

Common and Proper Nouns

Focus
- A **common noun** names a person, place, thing, or idea. Common nouns do not begin with a capital letter.

Example
dancer, country, car, color, happiness

- A **proper noun** names a *certain* person, place, or thing. Proper nouns begin with a capital letter.

Example
Dr. Green, America, English

Practice Underline the proper nouns in each sentence.

1. Mrs. Smith has a new baby girl.

2. The baby's name is Allison.

3. We went to see the baby at Riverside Hospital.

Underline the common nouns in each sentence.

1. My class is reading about being kind.

2. We must do one kind thing every day.

3. Today, I helped Mrs. Jones find her glasses.

Apply **Read the paragraph below. Underline with three lines the letters of proper nouns that need to be capitalized. Circle the common nouns.**

My name is melissa. I am a student at goshen lane elementary school. Right now, I am in the second grade and mr. sanchez is my teacher. My best friend, hillary, has a different teacher. We get to play together at recess. Every tuesday afternoon we have a music class together. School is a great place to learn new things and make great friends.

Read the common noun listed and write a proper noun to tell about yourself. Make sure to begin each proper noun with a capital letter.

Common Noun   **Proper Noun**

1. name   **1.** _____

2. where you live   **2.** _____

3. school   **3.** _____

4. teacher   **4.** _____

5. best friend   **5.** _____

Name _____ **Date** _____

/ō/ Sound and Spellings

Focus
- The /ō/ sound can be spelled with o and o__e.

Practice Replace the beginning letter of each word with one of the following letters to make a new rhyming word. Write the new word on the line. Use each letter one time.

j	d	r	w	m	s

1. no _____   4. don't _____

2. nose _____   5. host _____

3. home _____   6. poke _____

Use the pairs of words above to complete the following sentences. Write the words on the lines.

1. Use your _____ to smell the _____.

2. _____ parties will have a _____.

3. My mom said __ _____, _____ I can't go to the park.

4. The Eskimo's _____ is in the shape of a _____.

Apply   **Read the word in the box. Then read the sentence. Change the word in the box to make a new rhyming word that will complete the sentence. Write the word on the line.**

1. | cone | My dog loves to chew on his _____.

2. | toll | Mona put butter on the warm _____.

3. | fold | The man on the corner _____ hot dogs.

4. | role | We dug a _____ in the backyard.

5. | bolt | Suddenly, the train stopped with a _____.

6. | tone | Do you want an ice cream _____?

Circle the correct spelling of each word.

1.   sold   soled

2.   oveal   oval

3.   ow   owe

4.   hose   hos

5.   toen   tone

6.   cola   colea

Name _____ Date _____

/ū/ Sound and Spellings

Focus • The /ū/ sound can be spelled with a *u* or *u__e*.

Practice **Read each sentence. Circle the word that correctly completes the sentence.**

1. Mr. Baker will _____ me in math.
   tuteor   tutor

2. Mom took some _____ pictures of the baby.
   cute   cut

3. Florida is one of the _____ States.
   Uneited   United

4. I _____ to give up.
   refuse   refus

Circle the correct spelling of each word.

1. menu   menue

2. musice   music

3. cubea   cube

Apply

| tulip | flute | cupid | mule | huge | museum |

Write a sentence using each word above.

1. _____

_____

2. _____

_____

3. _____

_____

4. _____

_____

5. _____

_____

6. _____

_____

Phonics • *Skills Practice 1*

Name _____ **Date** _____

Selection Vocabulary

Focus

litter *n.* Scattered paper and other materials; trash.

witness *v.* To see or hear something.

dawn *n.* The time each morning at which daylight first begins.

engines *n.* Plural of **engine:** a machine that uses energy to run other machines.

glows *v.* Shines.

Practice **Write the vocabulary word that matches the definition below.**

1. _____ the time each morning at which daylight first begins

2. _____ to see or hear something

3. _____ scattered paper and other material

4. _____ shines

5. _____ machines that use energy to run other machines

Write a sentence that uses at least one vocabulary word.

Apply   Make a poster to let people know that it is important to take care of our Earth. Use at least three vocabulary words on your poster.

Name _____ Date _____

Recording Information

Many people have jobs that allow them to show kindness while they are working. Use the chart below to record jobs people do that show kindness and how the people doing these jobs show kindness.

Job	How does the person show kindness?
1.	1.
2.	2.
3.	3.
4.	4.
5.	5.

Summarizing and Organizing Information

Write a topic related to kindness that you want to find out more about.

List some things you already know about your topic.

What do you want to find out about your topic?

Find books, articles, or internet sites about your topic. Read them and write what you learn here. Use your own words.

Writing a Journal

 **Audience: Who** will read your journal?

_____

Purpose: What is your reason for writing a journal?

_____

Prewriting   **Plan your entries. Write down what you will include in your journal.**

> Write the date
> of each entry.

> Write what happens to you or
> what matters to you.

Write a list of possible journal topics. Have at least one topic about kindness. A few examples are given.

1. Write about something that made me happy yesterday.

2. Write about something that is important to me.

3. _____

4. _____

5. _____

Continue writing in your journal.

You can also include lists in your journal. Here are some kinds of lists you could write. Write your own ideas for more lists. Have at least one list about kindness.

1. Make a list of all the people I talked to yesterday.

2. Make a list of things I want to do on my birthday.

3. Make a list of my favorite books, television, shows, or movies.

4. _____

5. _____

6. _____

What are some good reasons for keeping a journal?

_____

_____

How could a journal help you?

_____

_____

Name _____ **Date** _____

Long o spelled *o* and *o_e*
Long u spelled *u* and *u_e*

Focus
- Long vowels sound like their names.
- Two ways long o can be spelled are *o* and *o_e*.
- Two ways long u can be spelled are *u* and *u_e*.

Word List
1. menu
2. nose
3. most
4. cure
5. joke
6. unit
7. vote
8. fuse
9. soda
10. mule

Challenge Words
11. comb
12. bugle
13. total
14. human
15. suppose

Practice Sort the spelling words under the correct heading.

long o spelled *o*

1. _____
2. _____

long o spelled *o_e*

3. _____
4. _____
5. _____

long u spelled *u*

6. _____
7. _____

long u spelled *u_e*

8. _____
9. _____
10. _____

Apply   **Consonant-Substitution Strategy** Replace the underlined letter or letters to create a spelling word. The new word will have the same spelling for the long o sound.

16.   <u>n</u>ote   + v = _____

17.   <u>h</u>ost   + m = _____

18.   <u>c</u>hose + n = _____

19.   <u>b</u>roke + j = _____

Visualization Strategy Circle the correct spelling for each spelling word. Write the correct spelling on the line.

20.   sodu   soda   _____

21.   menu   menyou   _____

22.   mule   myool   _____

23.   kyure   cure   _____

24.   phuse   fuse   _____

25.   unit   younet   _____

Name _____ **Date** _____

Action Verbs

Focus

- An **action verb** tells what someone is doing.

Example

We **played** in the park for two hours.

Practice **Circle the action verb in each sentence.**

1. Every Saturday, I play at the park.

2. I saw some broken swings and litter.

3. My family wanted to help.

4. Mom and Dad fixed the swings.

5. Grandma and I planted some flowers.

6. Then, we all cleaned up the litter.

7. Everyone said the park was beautiful.

8. How can you make the world a better place?

Apply **Read the paragraph below. Write an action verb from the box in each blank.**

pack	use	recycle	help	love
made	save	sort	putting	take

It is important for every person to _____. We can

_____ Earth and _____ energy. You can

_____ trash at home into paper, plastic, and metal

containers. New things can be _____ from these used

items. People can also _____ things in different ways

instead of _____ them in the trash. For example,

_____ your lunch in a reusable bag. You can also

_____ a cloth bag to the grocery store. There are

many ways to _____ our Earth.

Read the story below. Circle the best action verb for each sentence.

The first Earth Day   **happened   are**   in 1970. Every year on

April 22nd, people   **do   find**   things to   **use   help**   the Earth.

We should   **make   take**   every day Earth Day.

Name _____ **Date** _____

/ā/ and /ī/ Sound and Spelling

Focus
- The /ā/ sound can be spelled with *a* and *a__e*.
- The /ī/ sound can be spelled with *i* or *i__e*.

Practice Look back at "The Elves and the Shoemaker." Find one example of a word that uses each of the spelling patterns below. Write the word you find on the correct line.

a	*a__e*	*i*	*i__e*
_____	_____	_____	_____

Underline the spelling pattern in each word below. Draw a picture to illustrate each word.

1. paper   **2.** plane   **3.** spider   **4.** kite

Apply | Read the word in the box. Then read the sentence. Change the word in the box to make a new rhyming word that will complete the sentence. Write the word on the line. Underline the spelling pattern in each word you write.

1. [**kind**] I changed my _____ about the party.

2. [**crazy**] Our _____ cat sleeps all day.

3. [**same**] Would you like to play a _____ with me?

4. [**size**] I won first _____ in the contest.

5. [**hike**] Nelson does not _____ ice cream.

6. [**lady**] It is _____ under the tree.

7. [**grace**] Please put everything back in its _____.

8. [**mind**] Did Alice _____ her lost puppy?

Write a sentence using a word with each spelling pattern given. Underline the spelling pattern word in each sentence.

1. a _____

2. a__e _____

3. i _____

4. i__e _____

Name _____ Date _____

/ō/ and /ū/ Sound and Spellings

Focus

- The /ō/ sound can be spelled with an *o* and *o__e*.
- The /ū/ sound can be spelled with a *u* and *u__e*.

Practice Look back at "The Elves and the Shoemaker". Find one example of a word that uses each of the spelling patterns below. Write the word you find on the correct line.

o   *u*

_____   _____

Write a sentence using each word above.

1. _____

2. _____

Choose a word from the box below to complete each sentence. Write the word on the line.

perfume	tutu	rodeo	broke	excuse	pupil

1. I said, "_____ me," when I ran into her.

2. We saw horses, cowboys, and bulls at the _____.

3. The ballerina wore a pink _____.

4. Her _____ smelled like flowers.

5. When the vase fell on the floor, it _____.

6. Another name for a student is _____.

Read each hint. Fill in the vowel to complete the word.

1. a song two people sing together   d _____ et

2. to give something away   d _____ nate

3. opposite of open   cl _____ se

4. musical tones   n _____ tes

Name _____ Date _____

Selection Vocabulary

Focus

leather *n.* Material made from the skin of an animal.

shoemaker *n.* Someone who makes shoes.

elves *n.* Plural of **elf**: a type of a fairy.

finest *adj.* Nicest.

flash *n.* An instant.

Practice Complete the following crossword puzzle.

ACROSS

2 Material made from the skin of an animal

3 Very nice

4 An instant

5 Type of fairies

DOWN

1 Someone who makes shoes

Apply   **Circle the correct word that completes each sentence.**

1. My new shoes are made from _____.
   a. leather   **b.** usual   **c.** finest

2. There was a _____ of lightening during the storm.
   a. elves   **b.** flash   **c.** skipped

3. The _____ and his wife lived happily ever after.
   a. elves   **b.** shoemaker   **c.** midnight

4. Michael had the _____ pair of skates.
   a. leather   **b.** amazement   **c.** finest

5. _____ are in many fairytales.
   a. elves   **b.** shoemaker   **c.** cutomers

Draw a picture of the following vocabulary words.

1. *elves*   **2.** *shoemaker*   **3.** something that can *flash*   **4.** something made from *leather*

Name _____ **Date** _____

Sequence

- **Sequence** is the order in which things happen in a story. The more you know about when things happen in a story, the better you can understand the story.

- Some sequence clue words tell:

  the **order** in which things happen: *first, then, finally*

  the **time** or when things happen: *tonight, in the morning, once upon a time*

Practice **Look through "The Elves and the Shoemaker" for examples of sequence words.**

1. Circle the kind of sequence words the writer uses most often.

time   order

2. List two examples of sequence words or phrases from the story.

a. _____   **b.** _____

Underline the time and order words in each sentence.

1. Tomorrow, my class will talk about our pets.

2. First, I will tell my pet's name.

Apply | **Number the following events from the story in the sequence in which they happened.**

_____ When he awoke, the shoemaker found a pair of shoes on the table.

_____ One night, the shoemaker left his last piece of leather on a table.

_____ Once upon a time, there lived a shoemaker and his wife.

_____ For some time the shoemaker would leave leather and find shoes each morning.

_____ At midnight, they saw two elves making the shoes.

_____ When the elves found the clothes, they danced around.

_____ One night, the shoemaker and his wife hid to see who was making the shoes.

_____ Everyone lived happily ever after.

_____ Afterwards, the wife made the elves clothes to keep them warm.

Name _____ Date _____

Writing a Fairy Tale

Think **Audience: Who** will read your fairy tale?

_____

Purpose: What is your reason for writing a fairy tale?

_____

Prewriting Use this story map to plan your fairy tale.

Characters: (people in the story)	Setting: (where the story happens)

Plot (what happens)

Beginning: (problem)	Middle: (events)	Ending: (how problem is solved)

Revising Use this checklist to revise.

- ☐ Does your story have parts that make it a fairy tale?
- ☐ Are the setting, characters, and events imaginary?
- ☐ Is the problem solved with a happy ending?
- ☐ Do your words help the reader visualize what is happening?
- ☐ Did you use dialogue to make your story more interesting?

Editing/Proofreading Use this checklist to correct mistakes.

- ☐ Make sure to use proofreading symbols when editing.
- ☐ Is every word or special term spelled correctly?
- ☐ Did you capitalize character's names, places, and the beginning of sentences?
- ☐ Does every sentence end with the correct punctuation mark?
- ☐ Is the dialogue written correctly with quotation marks?

Publishing Use this checklist to prepare for publication.

- ☐ Give your fairy tale a title. Remember to underline your title.
- ☐ Write or type a neat copy.
- ☐ Include a drawing of an important character or event from your fairy tale.

Name _____ Date _____

Long vowel a spelled *a* and *a_e*
Long vowel i spelled *i* and *i_e*
Long vowel o spelled *o* and *o_e*
Long vowel u spelled *u* and *u_e*

Word List

1. label
2. vine
3. bonus
4. wild
5. gate
6. huge
7. zero
8. made
9. spoke
10. use

Focus
- Long vowels sound like their names.
- Long a can be spelled *a* and *a_e*.
- Long i can be spelled *i* and *i_e*.
- Long o can be spelled *o* and *o_e*.
- Long u can be spelled *u* and *u_e*.

Challenge Words

11. basic
12. program
13. usual
14. finest
15. caper

Practice Sort a spelling word into each pattern:

long a spelled *a*

1. _____

long a spelled *a_e*

2. _____

long o spelled *o*

3. _____

long o spelled *o_e*

4. _____

long i spelled *i_e*

5. _____

long u spelled *u_e*

6. _____

Apply **Rhyming Strategy** Write the spelling word that rhymes with each set of words below. The new word should have the same spelling pattern for the long vowel sound.

16. mine   shine   _____

17. choke   broke   _____

18. mate   rate   _____

19. shade   fade   _____

20. child   mild   _____

Proofreading Strategy Circle the misspelled words. Rewrite the words correctly below.

You should always read the laybel when you are choosing a food item. It's good to youz foods that have zeeroh grams of fat. Choosing the right foods can be a hyooj boanus for your health.

21. _____

22. _____

23. _____

24. _____

25. _____

Name _____ Date _____

Following Directions

Think of something you know how to do well. It may be a chore, a craft, or a game. Write the name of the task you do well here.

_____

What are the steps for your task? Write the steps below.

_____

_____

_____

_____

_____

Look over the steps. Are they in the correct order? Put numbers next to each step to show which is first, next, and so on.

Now write each step clearly in the correct order. Use complete sentences. Draw a picture to go with each step.

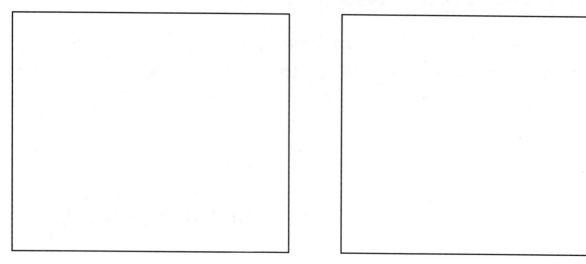

1. _____

   _____

   _____

2. _____

   _____

   _____

3. _____

   _____

   _____

4. _____

   _____

   _____

Name _____ Date _____

Helping and Linking Verbs

Focus
- Sometimes verbs don't show action. These verbs are called linking and helping verbs.
- A **linking verb** joins, or connects, the parts of a sentence to make it complete.

Example

    There **is** a pretty shell on the beach.

- A **helping verb** helps the main verb in a sentence tell when something will happen, has happened, or is happening.

Example

    We **are** planning to look for shells tomorrow.

Practice **Read each sentence. Write an *L* if the underlined verb is a linking verb. Write an *H* if the verb is a helping verb.**

1. I <u>was</u> swimming in the ocean today. _____

2. Fish <u>have been</u> swimming in the oceans for millions of years. _____

3. The fish <u>was</u> swimming by our boat. _____

4. There <u>is</u> a fish in the pond. _____

Apply **Read the paragraph below. Underline the linking verbs. Circle the helping verbs.**

There are more than 20,000 types of fish. I have eaten swordfish and sardines. Have you ever eaten eel? A shark is a very big fish. Are sea horses fish? The lionfish is orange.

Read the paragraph below. Write a linking or helping verb to complete each sentence.

There _____ six fish in my aquarium. The blue fish _____ swimming faster than the orange fish. My cat _____ watching them swim. I _____ tried to teach the cat to behave. These fish _____ not for dinner, Miss Kitty!

Grammar • *Skills Practice 1*

Name _____ Date _____

/ē/ Sounds and Spellings

Focus • The /ē/ sound can be spelled with e and e__e.

Practice Read each sentence. Circle the word with the /ē/ sound. Write e or e__e on the line for the spelling pattern of each word you circled.

1. Maybe Joe should go to the store alone. _____

2. Did you complete the homework? _____

3. Mom's birthday present is a secret. _____

Choose a word from the box that makes sense in the sentence. Write the word on the line.

1. Mrs. Jones showed us a math problem.

The answer was _____.

She _____ the board.

before
erased
zero

2. Jessica is typing on the computer.

She wants to _____ a word.

So, she presses the _____ key.

delete
the
remove

Apply Look at the pairs of words below. Choose the word that will complete the sentence. Write the word on the line.

1. Julia is sick and has a _____.
   (fever, fevr)

2. An _____ is someone who plays sports.
   (athlet, athlete)

3. Let's _____ to be pirates.
   (preteend, pretend)

4. _____ books belong to Keith.
   (These, Thes)

5. The sidewalk is made from _____.
   (concret, concrete)

6. _____ is visiting us from Mexico.
   (Hee, He)

7. It is fun to watch teams _____ in a basketball game.
   (compete, compet)

8. A sign in our yard says, "_____ of Dog!"
   (Beweare, Beware)

9. Can you _____ what you just said?
   (repeeat, repeat)

10. You can make the toy car move using the _____ control.
    (remeot, remote)

Phonics • *Skills Practice 1*

Name _____ **Date** _____

/ā/, /ī/, /ō/, /ū/ Sounds and Spellings Review

Focus
- The /ā/ sound can be spelled with *a* and *a__e*.
- The /ī/ sound can be spelled with *i* or *i__e*.
- The /ō/ sound can be spelled with an *o* and *o__e*.
- The /ū/ sound can be spelled with a *u* and *u__e*.

Practice Use the words in the box to complete each sentence. Write the words on the line.

| brave | attitude | bride | overalls | music | climb | mayor | robe |

1. We watched the _____ walk down the aisle.

2. A _____ has the job of running a city.

3. Keep a good _____ when playing games.

4. The farmer wore _____.

5. My brother loves to _____ on things.

6. Grandma always wears a red _____.

7. Kim tried to be _____ at the dentist.

8. Lucy danced to the _____.

Apply   Unscramble the following words and write the new word on the line. Underline the spelling pattern in each word.

1. t   o   e   n   _____

2. z   i   e   s   _____

3. y   s   a   h   k   _____

4. e   n   m   u   _____

5. l   a   o   t   t   _____

6. r   c   t   a   e   _____

7. t   i   y   n   _____

8. u   e   a   s   m   _____

Write the spelling pattern for the correct spelling on the line.

1. Ohio _____   5. usual _____

2. reduce _____   6. blame _____

3. hive _____   7. close _____

4. basic _____   8. tiny _____

Name _____ Date _____

Selection Vocabulary

Focus

snoozing *v.* Taking a quick nap.

raged *v.* Past tense of **rage**: to act violently.

furious *adj.* Very angry.

gnaw *v.* To chew.

repay *v.* To pay or give back.

Practice **Replace the underlined phrase with the correct vocabulary word.**

1. My uncle was <u>taking a quick nap</u> on the couch.

_____

2. The hamster began to <u>chew</u> on the toy.

_____

3. I promised to <u>pay</u> her <u>back</u> for the snack.

_____

4. Stanley was <u>very angry</u> that his pictures were ripped.

_____

5. The lion began to <u>act violently</u> in his cage.

_____

Apply   **Use your knowledge of the vocabulary words from this lesson to complete the following activities.**

1. Draw a picture of the character that was *snoozing* in the story.

2. What happened to make lion *furious*?

_____

3. Who *raged* in the story and why?

_____

4. How did mouse *repay* lion for letting him go?

_____

5. How was the word *gnaw* used in the story?

_____

6. Which two vocabulary words are similar? What makes them similar?

_____

Name _____ Date _____

Reality and Fantasy

> **Focus**
> - **Reality** is people, animals, and objects that are in the real word. The events could happen in the real world.
>
> Example
> My dog buried his bone in the yard.
>
> - **Fantasy** is when animals, people, and objects do things they could not do in the real world. The events in the story could not happen in the real world.
>
> Example
> My dog drew a map for his buried bone.

Practice Read each sentence below. Write an *R* if the sentence could really happen and an *F* if the sentence is a fantasy.

1. The library was closed today.   _____

2. Our new teacher is an alien.   _____

Change the sentence above that is fantasy to a realistic sentence. Change the sentence above that is a realistic sentence to a fantasy sentence.

1. _____   _____

2. _____

Look back at "The Lion and the Mouse". Write down the things In the story that are real and the things in the story that are fantasy. Write the examples in the correct box.

Reality

1. _____

2. _____

3. _____

4. _____

5. _____

Fantasy

1. _____

2. _____

3. _____

4. _____

5. _____

Name _____   Date _____

Writing an Action Tale

Think   **Audience: Who** will read your action tale?

_____

Purpose: What is your reason for writing an action tale?

_____

Prewriting   Use this story map to plan your action tale.

Characters: (people in the story)	Setting: (where the story happens)

Plot (what happens)

Beginning: (problem)	Middle: (events)	Ending: (how problem is solved)

Revising Use this checklist to revise.

☐ Does your story have a lot of action?

☐ Are the setting, characters, and events exciting?

☐ Is the problem solved?

☐ Are the events in sequence?

☐ Did you use time and order words?

Editing/Proofreading Use this checklist to correct mistakes.

☐ Did you use descriptive words?

☐ Is every word or special term spelled correctly?

☐ Did you capitalize character names, places, and the beginning of sentences?

☐ Does every sentence end with the correct punctuation mark?

Publishing Use this checklist to prepare for publication.

☐ Give your action tale a title. Remember to underline your title.

☐ Write or type a neat copy.

☐ Include a drawing of the most exciting part of your action tale.

Name _____ **Date** _____

Long e spelled e and e_e

Focus
- Long vowels sound like their names.
- Two ways long e can be spelled are e and e_e.

Practice **Sort the spelling words under the correct heading.**

long e spelled e

1. _____
2. _____
3. _____
4. _____
5. _____
6. _____

long e spelled e_e

7. _____
8. _____
9. _____
10. _____

Word List

1. repay
2. meter
3. eve
4. gene
5. beside
6. elect
7. pretend
8. these
9. hero
10. demand

Challenge Words

11. compete
12. create
13. evening
14. delete
15. eraser

Apply **Visualization Strategy** Circle the correct spelling for each spelling word. Write the correct spelling on the line.

16. uleckt   elect   _____

17. demand   dumand   _____

18. eeve   eve   _____

19. repay   reapay   _____

20. pretend   preatend   _____

Proofreading Strategy Circle the misspelled words. Rewrite the words correctly below.

What makes someone a hearoh? Is it a special jeen that they have? Is it someone who is really strong? No, theaz things do not matter. It could be someone who pays for your parking meatur when you are out of money, or someone who will sit buside you when you are hurt. Plain and simple, it is someone who helps you when you need it!

21. _____

22. _____

23. _____

24. _____

25. _____

Name _____ Date _____

Using Newspapers and Magazines

Find a story or article in a newspaper or magazine. Then answer the questions below.

Is your article from a newspaper or magazine?

_____

Name and date of newspaper or magazine:

_____

_____

Name of article and page it starts on:

_____

_____

How many pages is the article?

_____

What is the article about?

_____

_____

Write a short summary of your newspaper article. Use complete sentences.

_____

_____

_____

_____

Study Skills • *Skills Practice 1*

Name _____ **Date** _____

Subject and Predicate

Focus
- A sentence is a group of words that expresses a complete thought. A sentence has two parts: a naming part and a telling part.

- The **subject** of a sentence includes all the words in the naming part.

Example
The game of soccer

- The **predicate** includes all the words in the telling part.

Example
is played around the world.

Practice Underline the subject once and underline the predicate twice in each sentence.

1. Soccer began in England in the 1800s.

2. Two teams of 11 players each compete in soccer.

3. The players try to put a ball into the other team's goal.

4. The goals are two nets at opposite ends of a rectangular field.

5. Each goal is worth one point to the team that kicked the ball.

Apply **Write an *S* if the underlined part is a subject, and write a *P* if it is a predicate. Put an *S* or *P* on the blank line after each sentence.**

1. The game of rugby uses an oval shaped ball. _____

2. The players on a rugby team carry, kick, or pass the ball. _____

3. Fifteen players make up a team. _____

4. The object of the game is to score goals. _____

5. The team with the ball is the offensive team. _____

6. The game of football developed from the English game _____
   of rugby.

7. The team trying to stop the offensive team is the _____
   defensive team.

Write three sentences. Underline the subject once and the predicate twice.

1. _____

2. _____

3. _____

Grammar • *Skills Practice 1*

Name _____ Date _____

/n/ Sounds and Spellings

Focus
- The /n/ sound can be spelled with *kn*. When using *kn* together, the *k* is silent and you only hear the *n*.

Practice Add *kn* to the letters on the right to form a word. Write the word on the line and read it aloud.

1. *kn*   ee   _____

2. *kn*   it   _____

3. *kn*   ow   _____

4. *kn*   ife   _____

Apply Choose a word from the box below to complete each sentence. Write the word on the line.

| knock | knight | knelt | knack | known |

1. The _____ is wearing a suit of armor.

2. Allison has a _____ for drawing.

3. You should have _____ not to yell.

/r/ Sound and Spelling

Focus
• The /r/ sound can be spelled with *wr*. When using *wr* together, the *w* is silent and you only hear the *r*.

Practice **Write a rhyming word that begins with *wr* for each word given.**

1. song   _____

2. note   _____

3. list   _____

4. map   _____

5. neck   _____

Apply **Read each word or words. Write the word from above that you think of after reading the word or words.**

1. present   _____

2. not right   _____

3. hand and arm   _____

4. tense of write   _____

5. crash   _____

Name _____ Date _____

/f/ Sound and Spelling

Focus • The /f/ sound can be spelled with *ph*.

Practice Draw a picture of the word in the box.

1. elephant

2. telephone

Apply Choose the word that best completes the sentence and write the word on the line.

1. Grandma keeps a _____ of me in her bedroom.
(foto, photo)

2. The _____ has twenty-six letters.
(alfhabet, alphabet)

3. My best friend's name is _____.
(Ralph, Ralfe)

4. Write a _____ about kindness.
(paragraff, paragraph)

/m/ Sound and Spelling

Focus
- The /m/ sound can be spelled with *mb*. When using *mb* together, the *b* is silent and you only hear the *m*.

Practice Add the letters to the front of the *mb* spelling pattern to make a word. Write the new word on the line. *Letters do not have to go in the order they are written.

1. a   l   _____mb

2. o   c   _____mb

3. l   i   _____mb

4. r   c   u   _____mb

5. t   u   h   _____mb

Apply Write a sentence with each word above.

1. _____

2. _____

3. _____

4. _____

5. _____

Name _____ Date _____

Selection Vocabulary

Focus

escalator *n.* Moving stairs.

fastened *v.* Past tense of **fasten:** to button.

yanked *v.* Past tense of **yank:** to pull.

palace *n.* A large, fancy house.

dashing *v.* Running suddenly.

Practice Circle the vocabulary words in the word search.

```
F  W  T  I  V  N  E  S
A  A  E  S  C  P  M  W
L  P  S  R  O  M  Y  A
C  E  C  T  D  T  L  C
D  X  A  C  E  Q  V  P
P  T  L  D  H  N  A  O
A  I  A  N  M  P  E  M
L  G  T  U  F  U  E  D
A  I  O  O  L  J  I  Z
C  Z  R  B  H  Y  Y  K
E  M  R  E  P  Z  A  M
H  D  A  S  H  I  N  G
G  I  O  M  U  X  K  T
O  U  P  U  A  G  E  O
P  K  N  E  D  U  D  S
```

Apply **Tell whether the boldfaced definition that is given for the underlined word in each sentence below makes sense. Circle Yes or No.**

1. The <u>palace</u> has thirty rooms.
a large fancy house .... Yes   No

2. Paul <u>yanked</u> the thread on his shirt.
pulled .... Yes   No

3. We rode the <u>escalator</u> up to the third floor.
a large fancy house .... Yes   No

4. We saw the boy <u>dashing</u> toward the school bus.
being pleased with .... Yes   No

5. Lisa <u>fastened</u> the overalls.
buttoned .... Yes   No

Write a sentence with each vocabulary word.

1. _____

2. _____

3. _____

4. _____

5. _____

Name _____ Date _____

Making Inferences

Focus
- Sometimes a writer gives us hints about an event in the story or about what a character is thinking or feeling. These hints can help readers make **inferences**.
- A reader makes an **inference** by using information from the story and information the reader knows from his or her experience.

Practice   **Read page 180 of "Corduroy". Circle the sentence that is true.**

Corduroy hopes that a shopper will buy him.

Corduroy hopes that a shopper doesn't buy him.

What clues let you know:

_____

1. Lin was out of breath as she told the teacher about finding someone's glasses on the playground.

Clue: _____

What the clue tells you:

_____

Apply Write a paragraph about a game you like to play or a game you don't like to play without telling whether you like the game or not. Let your readers use the clues to figure out how you feel about the game.

Do you like the game you wrote about in the paragraph?

Read your paragraph to someone. Did they think you liked the game you wrote about?

Ask your partner the best clue in your paragraph that let them know how you felt about the game. Write the clue they told you.

Name _____ Date _____

Writing a Personal Narrative

Think **Audience: Who** will read your story?

_____

Purpose: What is your reason for writing your story?

_____

Prewriting In the left column, list a problem you have had. In the right column, list how you solved each problem.

Use the graphic organizer below to plan your narrative.

Problem:

Event 1:

Event 2:

Solution:

Revising Use this checklist to revise.

☐ Did you put events in the order that they took place?

☐ Do your ideas clearly show cause and effect of events that happen?

☐ Do you have a clear topic sentence?

☐ Did you correctly use time and order words?

☐ Does your interest or excitement show in the way you tell your story?

☐ Does your story have a beginning, middle, and end?

Editing/Proofreading Use this checklist to correct mistakes.

☐ Is every paragraph indented?

☐ Is every word or special term spelled correctly?

☐ Does every sentence start with a capital letter and end with correct punctuation?

Publishing Use this checklist to prepare for publication.

☐ Write or type a neat copy.

☐ Include a drawing, photographs, or a timeline to help tell about your writing.

Name _____ **Date** _____

/n/ spelled *kn*; /r/ spelled *wr*; /f/ spelled *ph* Long e spelled *e* and *e_e*

Focus
- One way the /n/ sound can be spelled is *kn*. The letter *k* is silent.
- One way the /r/ sound can be spelled is *wr*. The letter *w* is silent.
- One way the /f/ sound can be spelled is *ph*, as in the word *trophy*.
- Two ways the long e sound can be spelled are *e* and *e_e*.

Practice Sort the spelling words under the correct heading.

/n/ spelled *kn*
1. _____
2. _____
3. _____

/r/ spelled *wr*
4. _____
5. _____
6. _____

/f/ spelled *ph*
7. _____
8. _____
9. _____

long e spelled *e_e*
10. _____

Word List
1. wren
2. knot
3. knife
4. write
5. phone
6. graph
7. wrap
8. here
9. phase
10. knit

Challenge Words
11. alphabet
12. wrinkle
13. known
14. concrete
15. photo

Apply Meaning Strategy Circle the correct spelling for each word. Write the correct spelling on the line.

11. Could you help me (rap, wrap) this gift? _____

12. The string on my kite has a (knot, not) in it. _____

13. Let's (right, write) a letter to Grandma this week. _____

14. We have lived (here, hear) for ten years. _____

Visualization Strategy Look at each word below. If the word is spelled correctly, write "correct" on the line. If the word is misspelled, write the correct spelling on the line.

20. nit _____

21. graph _____

22. knife _____

23. ren _____

24. fone _____

25. phase _____

Name _____ **Date** _____

Using a Dictionary and Glossary

Dictionaries are books that include thousands of words and their meanings.

A **glossary** is a part of a book, usually at the end, that contains only words that are in that book.

About Dictionaries and Glossaries

1. The words are in alphabetical order.

2. The words are spelled correctly.

3. Each word is defined or given a meaning.

4. Guide words tell the first and last words on a page.

Look up the following words from "Corduroy" in the glossary of your **Student Reader** and in a dictionary. Write the guide words from each source.

1. sighed

glossary: _____   _____

dictionary: _____   _____

2. exclaimed

glossary: _____   _____

dictionary: _____   _____

Sometimes it is important to find a new word quickly in the dictionary. In your mind, divide the dictionary into three parts: a beginning, a middle, and an end. Words are found in different parts, depending on their first letter.

Locator Chart

A-F words   Beginning of the dictionary

G-Q words   Middle of the dictionary

R-Z words   End of the dictionary

In the space next to each word, write which part of the dictionary the word can be found. Use the Locator Chart to help you. The first one is done for you.

1. amazing _____

2. enormous _____

3. wandered _____

4. gasped _____

5. department _____

6. mountain _____

7. mattress _____

8. toppled _____

9. apartment _____

10. blinked _____

11. comfortable _____

12. sew _____

Name _____ Date _____

Capitalization: First Word of a Sentence

> **Focus**
> • Capital letters are used in many places. One place capital letters are used is at the beginning of a sentence.
>
> • A sentence always begins with a capital letter.
> Example
> **C**amping is fun. **H**ave you ever slept outside?

Practice **Underline the beginning letter of each sentence three times.**

did you know that the teddy bear is over one hundred years

old? this popular toy has been around longer than the electric

light, telephone, and motor car. november of 1902, President

Theodore Roosevelt was on a hunting trip and had the chance to

shoot a captured bear. he refused, saying "Spare the bear!" a

cartoon was drawn of this event and was put into the newspaper.

two shopkeepers, Morris and Rose Michtom, made a soft bear

that they called Teddy's Bear. the teddy bear was an overnight

success and still very popular today.

Apply Write a paragraph about your most special toy. After writing, go back and circle the first letter of each sentence. Make sure it is a capital letter.

Underline three times the letters that should be capital letters.

Dear Corduroy,

i think you are a very nice bear. lisa is very lucky to have you as her special friend. i bet you like living with Lisa. she takes good care of you. it was nice of her to fix your overalls. she also had your own bed ready and waiting for you. make sure to be a good friend to her as well.

Sincerely,

A Corduroy Fan

Grammar • *Skills Practice 1*

Name _____ Date _____

/ē/ Sound and Spellings

Focus • The /ē/ sound can be spelled with *ee* and *ea*.

Practice Read the following words aloud.

dream	green	cheat	pea
feet	keep	leak	peek

Write the words with the /ē/ sound spelled like *leaf*.

1. _____   3. _____

2. _____   4. _____

Write the words with the /ē/ sound spelled like *weed*.

1. _____   3. _____

2. _____   4. _____

Apply   Read the word in the box. Then read the sentence. Change the word in the box to make a new rhyming word to complete the sentence.

1. | hear | If it is _____ you can see through it.

2. | tree | If you don't have to pay, then it is

     _____.

3. | reach | If you want to find seashells, go to the

     _____.

4. | beep | If you're not giving it away, it's yours

     to _____.

5. | beam | If you are an athlete, you might

     be on a _____.

6. | week | If you are spying, you might sneak a

     _____.

7. | weed | If you want a flower to grow, you

     should plant a _____.

8. | peach | If something is up high, you'll have to

     _____ for it.

Name _____ _____ Date _____

/ē/ Sounds and Spellings

Focus • The /ē/ sound can be spelled with e and e_e.

Practice Read the words in the box. Choose the correct word to complete each sentence.

equal	eve	theme	eleven	stampede	begin

1. There was a _____ of running horses.

2. Everyone gets an _____
share of the candy.

3. Andrea will be _____ years old.

4. "Let's Explore" is the _____
of this unit.

5. The night before a special day is called the

_____.

6. Should I _____ reading?

Apply Read each sentence. Circle the word that correctly completes the sentence.

1. Kendra reads a story every _____.
   a. evening   **b.** eevenin   **c.** eavening

2. Did you _____ the homework?
   a. complet   **b.** compleet   **c.** complete

3. Shawn will _____ in the spelling bee.
   a. compeet   **b.** compete   **c.** compeate

4. _____ comes before the number one.
   a. Zero   **b.** Zeeroe   **c.** Zereo

5. I will _____ to her letter soon.
   a. reaply   **b.** repely   **c.** reply

6. _____ is my best friend.
   a. Steve   **b.** Steevee   **c.** Steave

7. Can you _____ what you said?
   a. reapeat   **b.** repeat   **c.** repet

8. Just take a deep breath and _____.
   a. relax   **b.** realax   **c.** releax

Name _____ Date _____

Selection Vocabulary

Focus

insects *n.* Plural of **insect**: a six-legged bug.

invade *v.* To enter without an invitation.

cocoon *n.* A case that protects an insect while it changes to an adult.

tunnels *n.* Plural of **tunnel**: an underground passageway.

enemies *n.* Plural of **enemy**: a person or thing that wants to hurt another.

Practice **Complete the crossword puzzle.**

Across

1. A six-legged bug

3. A case that protects an insect while it changes

4. To enter without an invitation

5. People or things that want to hurt another

Down

2. Underground passageways

Apply Complete each sentence with a vocabulary word and then answer the question.

| insects | cocoon | enemies | invade | tunnels |

1. All _____ have six legs and three body parts.

What is an example of an insect? _____

2. Ants must protect themselves from _____.

What is an enemy of an ant? _____

3. The underground passages are called _____.

Why do ants dig tunnels? _____

_____

4. A pupa ant grows inside a _____.

What is another animal that grows inside of a cocoon?

_____

5. Look out! Ants are going to _____ the picnic!

Why do you think ants would invade your picnic?

_____

Selection Vocabulary • *Skills Practice 1*

Name _____   Date _____

Author's Purpose

Focus

• Author's write for different reasons. Sometimes they want to give readers information. Sometimes they write to entertain.

• Writers *entertain* readers by including

- funny words or events

- exciting or familiar events

• Writers *inform* readers by including

- facts that can be proven

• Writers *persuade* readers by including

- their opinions

• Writers *explain* to readers how to do something by including

- the steps in the process

Practice Numbered below are some titles of stories. A list of purposes that authors can use is in the box. Choose the one that fits each title.

| entertain | inform | persuade | explain |

1. "Why the School Year Should Be Longer"

_____

2. "The Great Mahooleywhazit and the Big YUCK!"

_____

3. "How to Feed a Baby"

_____

4. "Ocean Animals"

_____

Apply Answer the following questions.

What is the author's purpose of "Ants! They are Hard Workers!"?

_____

Write a reason for your answer.

_____

Name _____ Date _____

Recording Observations

After going on your nature walk, think about the different things that you observed. Write down these things under the correct category: *Living Things* or *Nonliving Things*.

Living Things

1. _____

2. _____

3. _____

4. _____

5. _____

Nonliving Things

1. _____

2. _____

3. _____

4. _____

5. _____

How can you tell if something is living or nonliving?

Look around the classroom. Write examples of three living and three nonliving things.

Living Things

1. _____

2. _____

3. _____

Nonliving Things

1. _____

2. _____

3. _____

Name _____ Date _____

Writing a Descriptive Paragraph

Think Audience: **Who** will read your paragraph?

_____

Purpose: **What** is your reason for writing your paragraph?

_____

Prewriting Your answers below will help you write your description.

1. What did you see?

_____

2. What did you feel to the touch?

_____

3. What did you smell?

_____

4. What did you hear?

_____

5. What did you taste?

_____

Revising — Use this checklist to revise.

- ☐ Do you have a clear topic sentence?
- ☐ Do your other sentences support the topic sentence?
- ☐ Do the words you use give a good description?
- ☐ Could you change any words to be more descriptive?
- ☐ Is there anything else you want to add to your paragraph?

Editing/Proofreading — Use this checklist to correct mistakes.

- ☐ Is the paragraph indented?
- ☐ Make sure all of your sentences are complete.
- ☐ Is every word or special term spelled correctly?
- ☐ Does every sentence start with a capital letter and end with correct punctuation?

Publishing — Use this checklist to prepare for publication.

- ☐ Write or type a neat copy.
- ☐ Include a drawing of your topic.

Name _____ **Date** _____

Long e spelled ee, ea, e, e_e

Focus The long e sound can be spelled many ways. Some of the ways it can be spelled are: *ee, ea, e, and e_e.*

Word List
1. real
2. sleep
3. we
4. feel
5. east
6. green
7. team
8. belong
9. knee
10. clear

Challenge Words
11. peach
12. cheese
13. please
14. between
15. eagle

Practice Sort the spelling words under the correct heading.

Long e spelled *ee*

1. _____
2. _____
3. _____
4. _____

Long e spelled *ea*

5. _____
6. _____
7. _____
8. _____

Long e spelled *e*

9. _____
10. _____

Apply Pronunciation Strategy Underline the letters that spell the long e sound in each word as you pronounce them. Then, write the spelling word with the same spelling of the long e sound as each set of words below.

11. beat   steam   _____

12. reed   sheep   _____

13. me   become   _____

14. been   steel   _____

15. fear   meal   _____

Visualization Strategy Circle the correct spelling for each word. Then write the correct spelling on the line.

16. slepe   sleep   _____

17. team   teme   _____

18. feel   feal   _____

19. wea   we   _____

20. eeste   east   _____

Name _____ **Date** _____

Summarizing and Organizing Information

Focus
- Writing a **summary** helps you organize the information from a piece of writing.
- A **summary** tells the *main idea* and *main points* of a longer piece of writing.

Practice
Write a topic related to the natural world that you want to find out more about.

List some things you already know about your topic.

_____

Who: _____

What: _____

When: _____

Where: _____

Why: _____

How: _____

UNIT 2 Lesson 1

Apply Find books or magazines about your topic. Read them and write what you learn here. Use your own words.

Who: _____

What: _____

_____

When: _____

_____

_____

Where: _____

_____

How: _____

_____

Other information: _____

_____

_____

_____

_____

Name _____   Date _____

Complete and Incomplete Sentences

Focus

- A **complete sentence** has a subject and a predicate.

- In an **incomplete sentence**, or **fragment**, the subject or predicate is missing.

- A **run-on sentence** is two ideas mixed together.

- To *correct* an **incomplete sentence**, add the missing subject or predicate to the sentence.

Example

    Fragment: Over one billion vehicles

    Correct: Over one billion vehicles have crossed the bridge.

- To correct a **run-on sentence**, write two sentences.

Example

    Run-On: The fog covers the bridge it stands over the water.

    Correct: The fog covers the bridge. It stands over the water.

UNIT 2 — Lesson 1

Practice Write *C* for complete sentence, *F* for fragment, or *R* for run-on.

1. Orange trees plenty of water. _____

2. Potatoes grow in cool climates they can't grow in freezing

weather. _____

3. My family likes to have a garden. _____

Rewrite each sentence correctly.

1. _____

2. _____

3. _____

Apply Circle the word group that correctly completes each sentence.

1. The first bridges   **were tree trunks.**
                            some footbridges.

2. Pontoon bridges   **the surface.**
                            float on the water.

3. Arches   **are very strong.**
                            curved supports.

Name _____   **Date** _____

/ā/ Sound and Spellings

Focus
- The /ā/ sound can be spelled with *ai_* and *_ay*.
- The *ai_* pattern is usually in the front or middle of a word.
- The *_ay* pattern is usually found at the end of a word.

Practice   Read the following words aloud.

aim	paint	okay	display
rain	away	waist	today

Write the words with the /ā/ sound spelled like *aid*.

1. _____   3. _____

2. _____   4. _____

Write the words with the /ā/ sound spelled like *way*.

1. _____   3. _____

2. _____   4. _____

Apply Choose a word from the box to complete each sentence. Write the word on the line.

bait	braid	holiday	sway	explain
away	wait	spray	daisy	maybe

1. What is your favorite _____?

2. Can you _____ my hair?

3. The teacher will _____ the assignment.

4. Linda put _____ on her fishing hook.

5. Grandpa picked a _____ for me.

6. I can't _____ to go to the circus.

7. Everyone needs to put the toys _____.

8. _____ we should eat lunch now.

9. I saw a tree _____ in the breeze.

10. Don't forget to _____ water on the plant.

Name _____ Date _____

/ā/ Sound and Spellings

Focus • The /ā/ sound can be spelled with *a* and *a_e*.

Practice Unscramble the following words. Write the word on the line and write *a* or *a_e* to tell the spelling pattern.

1. a p e r p   _____ _____

2. l a p e t   _____ _____

3. a y z l   _____ _____

4. r e d a t   _____ _____

5. s l e a c   _____ _____

6. c b e l a   _____ _____

Write a sentence using a word with each spelling pattern from above.

_____

_____

Apply **Choose a word from the box that makes sense in the sentence. Write the word on the line.**

1. Breakfast is the most important meal of the day.

   This morning, I _____ oatmeal.

   I also had a piece of _____.

table
bacon
ate

2. We went to the bakery Saturday morning.

   Mom let me _____ a doughnut.

   Then, I ate a _____.

bagel
pastry
taste

3. Reading is my favorite thing to do.

   My teacher is reading a _____.

   It is about a sneaky _____.

fable
snake
movie

4. A newspaper has a lot of interesting stories.

   My family gets the _____ paper.

   The front _____ stories
   are interesting.

story
page
daily

Name _____ Date _____

Selection Vocabulary

Focus

chain *n.* A row of connected or related circles.

fossil *n.* Preserved remains.

trace *v.* To follow the path of something.

outstretched *adj.* Reaching out.

print *n.* A mark made by pressing.

Practice **Match each word on the left to its definition on the right.**

1. fossil

2. trace

3. outstretched

4. chain

5. print

a. a row of connected or related circles

b. preserved remains

c. a mark made by pressing

d. to follow the path of something

e. reaching out

Write two sentences using at least one vocabulary word in each sentence.

1. _____

2. _____

UNIT 2 Lesson 2

Apply   **Use the vocabulary words to complete each sentence.**

chain	trace	print	fossil	outstretched

1. The dog's collar was connected to a _____.

2. I saw a _____ at the museum.

3. _____ the letter with your finger.

4. Brandi made a leaf _____.

5. His arm was _____ to reach the light.

Write the vocabulary word you think of after reading each word or words.

1. leaf or shell   _____

2. circles   _____

3. follow   _____

4. remains   _____

5. reaching   _____

Selection Vocabulary • *Skills Practice 1*

Name _____ **Date** _____

Compare and Contrast

Focus
- To **compare** means to tell how things, events, or characters are alike in some way.

- To **contrast** means to tell how things, events, or characters are **different**.

- **Clue words** help show how things are alike and different.

Clue Words

Alike		**Different**
both	as	different
same	too	but
like		

Practice Circle whether the sentence is comparing or contrasting. Write the clue word on the line.

1. Uncle Joe has a collection of rocks, just like me.

   compare   contrast   _____

2. Our collections are very different in size.

   compare   contrast   _____

Apply Use the chart below to compare an apple and a banana. Write three ways these foods are alike and three ways that they are different.

Apple and Banana

Compare (alike)	Contrast (different)
1. _____	1. _____
_____	_____
2. _____	2. _____
_____	_____
3. _____	3. _____
_____	_____

Use the lists above to help you write a sentence to compare these things and a sentence to contrast them. Underline the clue word used in each sentence.

Compare

_____

Contrast

_____

Name _____ Date _____

Writing a Comparison

 **Think** **Audience: Who** will read your comparison?

_____

Purpose: What is your reason for writing your comparison?

_____

 **Prewriting** Use this Venn diagram to organize your compare and contrast paragraphs.

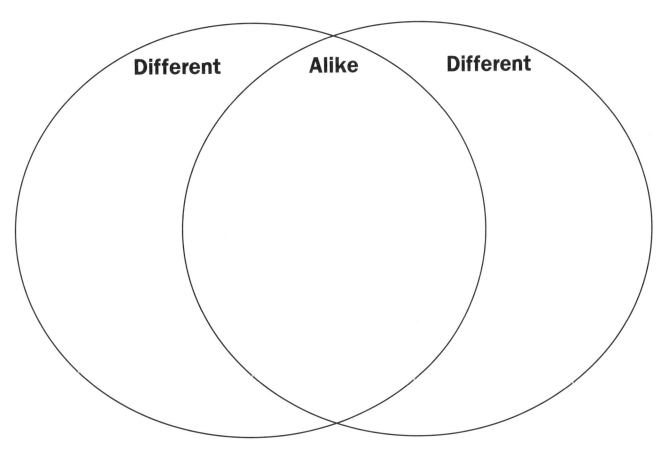

Revising Use this checklist to revise.

- ☐ Did you include a topic sentence that names the two stories?
- ☐ Did you compare and contrast the two stories?
- ☐ Does the first paragraph compare the stories?
- ☐ Does the second paragraph begin with a transition sentence?
- ☐ Does the second paragraph contrast the stories?
- ☐ Did you use clue words?
- ☐ Will the reader understand the information?

Editing/Proofreading Use this checklist to correct mistakes.

- ☐ Is each paragraph indented?
- ☐ Make sure all of your sentences are complete.
- ☐ Is every word or special term spelled correctly?
- ☐ Does every sentence start with a capital letter and end with correct punctuation?

Publishing Use this checklist to prepare for publication.

- ☐ Write or type a neat copy.
- ☐ Include a drawing of the two things in the comparison.

Name _____ Date _____

Long vowel a spelled *ai_*, *_ay*, *a*, and *a_e*

Focus
- Long vowel a sounds like the letter a.
- Some ways that the long a sound can be spelled are *ai_*, *_ay*, *a*, and *a_e*.

Practice **Sort the spelling words under the correct heading.**

long a spelled *ai_*

1. _____
2. _____
3. _____

long a spelled *_ay*

4. _____
5. _____
6. _____

long a spelled *a*

7. _____
8. _____

long a spelled *a_e*

9. _____
10. _____

Word List
1. stay
2. rain
3. base
4. April
5. May
6. chain
7. trace
8. play
9. paid
10. fable

Challenge Words
11. waist
12. railroad
13. pavement
14. flavor
15. Thursday

Rhyming Strategy Write the spelling word that rhymes with each set of words below. The new word should have the same spelling pattern for the long a sound.

11. day   ray   _____

12. cable   stable   _____

13. fair   chair   _____

14. chase   case   _____

15. main   stain   _____

Proofreading Strategy Circle the misspelled words. Rewrite the words correctly below.

One of my favorite months is the month of Mai. In the month of Ayprul, there is always a lot of rayn, so you must plai indoors. Once May comes, I like to do outdoor activities, like making a daisy chane. I cannot wait for next May to come!

16. _____

17. _____

18. _____

19. _____

20. _____

Name _____ Date _____

Using the Card Catalog

Focus
- The **card catalog** is a system for finding books in the library.
- Every catalog card has a call number, the name of the book, the author's name, a summary, and a cross-reference.

Practice Find and mark these items on the card catalog card shown:
  - **Circle the call number.**
  - **Draw a line under the author's name.**
  - **Draw two lines under the subject.**
  - **Put a check mark by the title.**

[E
599.74422BEN]
Bender, Lionel
Lions and Tigers
New York, Gloucester Press, c. 1988
    [31] p.
Summary: Describes the habits and behaviors of lions and
         tigers, with a discussion of how they survive.
1. lions   2. tigers

Apply Use the card or computer catalog to find one book on a subject you are interested in. Write the call number, the author's name, and the book title on the lines below. Then take the paper with you as you look for the book.

Call Number: _____

Author's Name: _____

Book Title: _____

Answer the following questions.

1. Did you find the book? _____

2. Did you find the information from the card catalog helpful?

Why? _____

_____

_____

3. Why do you think the card catalog is important to have

in a library? _____

_____

_____

Name _____ Date _____

Kinds of Sentences

Focus
- There are different kinds of sentences.
- A **declarative sentence** makes a statement. It always ends with a period (.).

Example
> Mars is a planet.

- An **interrogative sentence** asks a question. It always ends in a question mark (?).

Example
> Will people ever live on Mars?

- An **imperative sentence** gives directions or a command. It always ends in a period (.).

Example
> Begin the countdown now.

- An **exclamatory sentence** shows strong feelings. It always ends in an exclamation mark (!).

Example
> What a perfect launch!

Practice Read each sentence below. Write the type of sentence on the line.

1. Pick up that rock. _____

2. Did you find any rocks today? _____

Name _____ Date _____

End Marks

Focus

- Every sentence needs to end with a punctuation, or **end mark**.

- A statement or direction should end with a **period** (.).

Example

   It will rain today.

- A question should end with a **question mark** (?).

Example

   Do you have an umbrella?

- A sentence that shows strong feelings should end with an **exclamation point** (!).

Example

   Look out for that puddle!

Practice **Put the correct end mark at the end of each sentence.**

1. Where does snow come from

2. Icy droplets of water in clouds turn into snowflakes

3. It's amazing that no two snowflakes are alike

4. Where do the water droplets come from

5. They come from Earth's lakes, rivers, and oceans

Name _____ Date _____

/ē/ Sound and Spellings

Focus
- The /ē/ sound can be spelled with ee, ea, e, and e_e.

Practice Underline the /ē/ spellings in the words below. Some words have two spellings for /ē/.

1. repeat

2. between

3. legal

4. seaweed

5. delete

6. complete

7. remove

8. extreme

9. reheat

10. depend

Apply Choose the word that completes each sentence. Write the word on the line.

1. I can't _____ it! The snow _____
(behave, believe)   (keeps, peak)

falling and falling. The _____ look
(trees, only)

really pretty. Mom said _____ we
(these, maybe)

can go sledding.

2. Antoine can't _____ what to do. The
(decide, delay)

talent show is only two _____ away.
(weekly, weeks)

Antoine can juggle _____ bags.
(bean, beet)

He also does a _____ show with his
(pretend, the)

_____ puppet. Which would
(theme, zebra)

_____ better?
(me, be)

Name _____   Date _____

/ā/ Sound and Spellings

Focus •The /ā/ sound can be spelled with *ai_*, *_ay*, *a*, and *a_e*.

Practice **Read the word in the box. Then read the sentence. Change the word in the box to make a new rhyming word to complete the sentence.**

1. | same | The opposite of *wild* is _____.

2. | say | Mixing black and white makes _____.

3. | fair | Shoes come in a _____.

4. | hay | The waiter carried a big _____.

5. | whale | The store is having a _____.

6. | cage | Turn the _____ and keep reading.

7. | gain | Let's ride the _____ into the city.

8. | sway | We like to _____ kickball at recess.

9. | save | A _____ washed away our sandcastle.

10. | stair | Jamal sat in a _____ at the front of the room.

Apply   **Read each sentence. Circle the word that correctly completes the sentence.**

1. James wants to _____ the leaves into a big pile.
   a. rake   **b.** rayke   **c.** rak

2. If the _____ doesn't stop, we can play inside.
   a. raine   **b.** rane   **c.** rain

3. We made _____ pots in art class.
   a. claye   **b.** clay   **c.** claye

4. The _____ is locked each night at 9:00.
   a. gayt   **b.** gate   **c.** gait

5. Do you like red or green _____?
   a. grapes   **b.** graips   **c.** graypes

6. A monkey has a _____, but an ape does not.
   a. tayl   **b.** tail   **c.** taile

7. Mother's Day is in the month of _____.
   a. Mai   **b.** Mae   **c.** May

8. A _____ of black horses pulled the wagon.
   a. payr   **b.** pair   **c.** pare

9. We cannot _____ on the sidewalk.
   a. skat   **b.** skait   **c.** skate

10. Get a pump to _____ the flat tire.
    a. inflate   **b.** inflait   **c.** inflat

Name _____ Date _____

Selection Vocabulary

Focus

sensing *v.* Feeling.

dull *adj.* Not bright or clear.

antenna *n.* An insect feeler.

cycle *n.* A repeated sequence of events.

fussy *adj.* Hard to please.

Practice **Choose a vocabulary word from above that matches each definition.**

1. _____ hard to please

2. _____ not bright or clear

3. _____ feeling

4. _____ a repeated sequence of events

5. _____ an insect feeler

Apply **Circle the word in parentheses that best fits each sentence.**

1. Keith is not (fussy, dull) about the food he eats.

2. Different animals can (antennae, sense) danger.

3. (Dull, Sensing) colors can help some insects hide.

4. Count the (cycle, antennae) on the grasshopper's head.

5. Explain a grasshopper's life (cycle, fussy).

Draw a picture of a grasshopper. Write three sentences about a grasshopper using at least one vocabulary word in each sentence.

1. _____

2. _____

3. _____

Name _____ **Date** _____

Writing a Summary

Think **Audience: Who** will read your summary?

_____

Purpose: What is your reason for writing your summary?

_____

Prewriting Use the graphic organizer to organize the notes for your summary.

Topic:

Subtopic:	Subtopic:	Subtopic:	Subtopic:

Conclusion:

Revising Use this checklist to revise.

☐ Did you tell the main idea and details?

☐ Did you use your own words?

☐ Is there information that is not from the book or article?

☐ Will the reader understand the information?

☐ Did you write a conclusion to your summary?

Editing/Proofreading Use this checklist to correct mistakes.

☐ Make sure all of your sentences are complete.

☐ Is every word or special term spelled correctly?

☐ Does every sentence start with a capital letter and end with correct punctuation?

Publishing Use this checklist to prepare for publication.

☐ Write or type a neat copy.

☐ Add a photograph or drawing.

Name _____ **Date** _____

Long vowel a spelled *ai_, _ay, a, a_e*
Long vowel e spelled *ee, ea, e, e_e*

Focus
- Long vowels sound like their names.
- Long a can be spelled *ai_, _ay, a,* and *a_e*.
- Long e can be spelled *ee, ea, e,* and *e_e*.

Word List
1. tail
2. reach
3. queen
4. fear
5. say
6. gave
7. sweet
8. acorn
9. player
10. even

Challenge Words
11. underneath
12. always
13. depend
14. wait
15. sneeze

Practice **Sort the spelling words under the correct heading.**

long a spelled *ai_*

1. _____

long a spelled *_ay*

2. _____

3. _____

long a spelled *a*

4. _____

long a spelled *a_e*

5. _____

long e spelled *ee*

6. _____

7. _____

long e spelled *ea*

8. _____

9. _____

long e spelled *e_e*

10. _____

Apply Consonant-Substitution Strategy Replace the underlined letter to create a spelling word. Then write the new word.

11. <u>s</u>ail + *t* = _____

12. swee<u>p</u> + *t* = _____

13. <u>b</u>each + *r* = _____

14. sa<u>d</u> + *y* = _____

15. <u>t</u>ear + *f* = _____

Visualization Strategy Circle the correct spelling for each spelling word. Write the correct spelling on the line.

16. eavun   even   _____

17. queen   qween   _____

18. gave   gav   _____

19. playur   player   _____

20. acorn   akorn   _____

Name _____ Date _____

Table of Contents/Index

Focus
- You can find all kinds of important information in books when you know where to look.
- The **Table of Contents** is located in the front of a book. It is an organized list of the chapters and their page numbers.
- An **Index** is located in the back of a book. It is a detailed list of important words and phrases from the book. The words are in alphabetical order and a page number is included.

Practice **Find a partner and decide on a book to use for the following activities.**

1. Write the title of the book you chose.

_____

2. How many chapters are in this book?

_____

3. Choose one topic from this book and write down the page numbers where it can be found in the book.

_____

Apply **Use the table of contents and the index in books to help you find the information you are looking for. Do the following:**

- First, find a book on your subject.

- Then look in the table of contents. Find a chapter that may have information you need.

- Write the chapter title and the page number below. If you find more than one chapter with information you need, write the title and page number of each.

- Think of words that name the information you are looking for. Then look through the index of the book. Find words related to your subject. Write the page numbers.

Book Title: _____

Title of chapters and page numbers with information I need:

_____ Page: _____

_____ Page: _____

Words related to the information I'm looking for and the page numbers from the index:

_____ Page: _____

_____ Page: _____

Name _____ Date _____

Capitalization: Proper Nouns, Titles, and Initials

Focus
- There are many places to use capital letters.
- A **proper noun** names a particular person, place, or thing. A proper noun always begins with a capital letter.

Example
> **Alaska** is the biggest state in the **United States**.

- **Titles** in people's names begin with capital letters.

Example
> **Mr.** Tilly told us to form a straight line.
> **Dr.** Jilly gave me a checkup today.

- **Initials** from people's names are capitalized.

Example
> **E.B.** White is the author of *Stuart Little*.

Practice Underline three times each title or set of initials that should be capitalized in the sentence below.

1. John adams and John q. adams were both presidents of the united states of america.

2. The president of the united states is called mr. President.

3. Presidents t. roosevelt and franklin d. Roosevelt were cousins.

Apply   **Write an initial or title in the blank.**

1. Our family doctor is _____.

2. The soccer coach at our school is _____ Watson.

3. The gorilla at the zoo was named _____ Big.

4. The vet who takes care of our cats is named

   _____.

5. Did you ever see Jeff's dad, _____?

Read the story below. Underline three times all the titles of people and all the initials that should be capitalized. Use proofreading marks.

The architect i. m. pei was born in china in

1917. mr. pei has designed many large, beautiful

buildings. In 1960, he designed the terminal at

jfk international airport in new york. A landscape

architect designs gardens and outdoor spaces. The

first person to call himself a landscape architect

was f. l. olmsted.

Name _____ Date _____

/ē/ Sound and Spellings

Focus
- The /ē/ sound can be spelled with _ie_, _y, and _ey.

- The _ie_ pattern is usually found in the middle of a word, but can sometimes be at the end of the word.

- The _y and _ey patterns are usually found at the end of a word.

Practice **Read each word. Underline the spelling pattern used in each word.**

1. shield   **4.** many

2. alley   **5.** valley

3. pretty   **6.** grief

Choose one of the spelling patterns listed to complete each word. Write the pattern in the word and then write the word on the blank line.

1. lad_____   _____

2. ch___   ___f   _____

3. donk_____   _____

Apply **Read the sentence. Choose the word that completes the sentence. Write the word on the line.**

1. The _____ stole the diamond ring.
   thief   thefe   theyfe

2. My glass of milk is now _____.
   emptie   empty   emptee

3. We watched the _____ eat a banana.
   monkie   monkee   monkey

4. There are flowers growing in the _____.
   feeld   field   feyld

5. How much _____ is in the piggy bank?
   money   monie   mony

6. A four leaf clover is a _____ thing to find.
   lucky   luckie   luckey

7. I get a lot of _____ when it is Halloween.
   candee   candy   candie

8. Bees keep _____ in their hive.
   honie   hony   honey

9. Can I have a _____ of cake?
   piece   peyce   pyce

10. Will you read a _____ to me?
    storie   storey   story

Name _____ Date _____

/ē/ Sound and Spellings

Focus • The /ē/ sound can be spelled with ee, ea, e, and e_e.

Practice Underline the spelling pattern used in each word. Write the pattern and a new word with the same spelling pattern. The words do not have to rhyme.

1. screen   _____   _____

2. device   _____   _____

3. heat   _____   _____

4. feel   _____   _____

5. concrete   _____   _____

6. sneeze   _____   _____

7. recent   _____   _____

8. teach   _____   _____

9. even   _____   _____

10. speak   _____   _____

UNIT 2 Lesson 4

Apply Choose a word from the box to complete each sentence. Write the word on the line.

fifteen	seasons	pretending	here
tepee	evening	disappear	weeds

1. Winter, Spring, Summer, and Autumn are the four

_____.

2. We are _____ to be princesses.

3. Did you put the flashlight over _____?

4. The number after fourteen is _____.

5. Hannah and Jack pulled the _____
from the garden.

6. My friends and I made a _____ in my yard.

7. Is the play this _____?

8. The magician made the coin _____.

Phonics • *Skills Practice 1*

Name _____ Date _____

Selection Vocabulary

Focus

rent *n.* A regular payment for the right to use equipment or property that belongs to someone else.

deserted *v.* Past tense of **desert**: to leave something behind.

vacant *adj.* Empty.

tenants *n.* Plural of **tenant**: one who lives in or on another person's property.

examined *v.* Past tense of **examine**: to look at closely and carefully.

Practice **Circle the correct word that completes each sentence.**

1. When no one lived in the birdhouse, it was _____.
   a. examined   **b.** vacant   **c.** rent

2. Mr. Chickadee _____ the house closely.
   a. examined   **b.** deserted   **c.** vacant

3. The sign said "Birdhouse for _____".
   a. tenants   **b.** deserted   **c.** rent

4. Mrs. Chickadee stayed outside and _____ her eggs.
   a. deserted   **b.** rent   **c.** tenants

Write the word from the word box that best matches the underlined word or phrase in the sentence below.

rent	vacant	examined	desert	tenants

1. Each month Bob pays <u>a regular payment for the right to use personal property</u> to the owner of his house.

   _____

2. Patty <u>looked at closely and carefully</u> the diamond ring.

   _____

3. We looked around the <u>empty</u> house.

   _____

4. The cat was forced to <u>leave behind</u> her kittens.

   _____

5. A chipmunk does not make a good <u>someone who lives in or on another person's property</u>.

   _____

Name _____ **Date** _____

Author's Point of View

- When a story is told by a character in the story, readers see the story through the eyes of that character. The author uses words like *I*, *me*, *mine*, *us*, *our*, and *we*. This is called **first-person point of view.**

- When the story is told by someone who is not part of the story, then the author uses words like *he*, *she*, *it*, *her*, *they*, and *their*. This is called **third-person point of view.**

Practice Circle the word that gives a clue about the author's point of view. Then write first-person point of view or third-person point of view.

1. Marsha and her mother almost missed the plane. They had a hard time getting a taxi to the airport. Luckily, their plane was late taking off.

   Point of view: _____

2. Jamie and I shared our snacks. Dad gave us apples, sandwiches, and peanuts. We ate the snacks at the picnic table.

   Point of view: _____

Apply Look at the story "Birdhouse For Rent".
What is the point of view?

_____

How do you know?

_____

Who is telling the story?

_____

Find an example in which the storyteller shares thoughts and feelings. Write it below.

_____

_____

Write a short sentence about something that happened in school from a first-person point of view. Then rewrite the sentence from a third-person point of view.

1. _____

2. _____

Name _____ Date _____

Writing a Comparison

Think **Audience: Who** will read your comparison?

_____

Purpose: What is your reason for writing your comparison?

_____

Prewriting Compare two animals of your choice. Use the Venn diagram to organize your ideas.

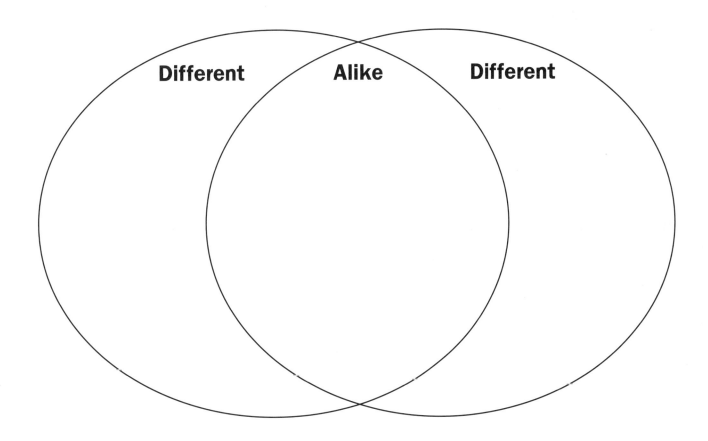

Different   **Alike**   **Different**

Revising   Use this checklist to revise.

☐ Did you clearly compare and contrast two animals?

☐ Does your writing contain facts about your topic?

☐ Did you use clue words to compare and contrast?

☐ Does the first paragraph compare the animals?

☐ Does the second paragraph begin with a transition sentence?

☐ Does the second paragraph contrast the animals?

☐ Will the reader understand the information?

Editing/Proofreading   Use this checklist to correct mistakes.

☐ Is each paragraph indented?

☐ Make sure all of your sentences are complete.

☐ Is every word or special term spelled correctly?

☐ Does every sentence start with a capital letter and end with correct punctuation?

Publishing   Use this checklist to prepare for publication.

☐ Write or type a neat copy.

☐ Include your diagram and pictures of the two animals.

Name _____ Date _____

The /s/ sound spelled *ce* and *ci_*
The /j/ sound spelled *ge* and *gi_*

Focus
- Two ways that the /s/ sound can be spelled are *ce* and *ci_*.
- Two ways that the /j/ sound can be spelled are *ge* and *gi_*.

Practice **Sort the spelling words under the correct heading.**

/s/ spelled *ce*

1. _____

2. _____

3. _____

/s/ spelled *ci_*

4. _____

5. _____

/j/ spelled *ge*

6. _____

7. _____

8. _____

/j/ spelled *gi_*

9. _____

10. _____

Word List
1. age
2. peace
3. pencil
4. magic
5. ice
6. digit
7. face
8. gem
9. circus
10. large

Challenge Words
11. piece
12. gentle
13. tragic
14. century
15. excite

Apply **Meaning Strategy** Write the spelling word next to its meaning clue.

11. Something that you write with _____

12. A feeling of calm and quiet _____

13. Frozen water _____

14. How old someone is _____

15. Another way to say "very large" _____

Visualization Strategy Circle the correct spelling for each spelling word. Write the correct spelling on the line.

16. serkus   circus   _____

17. face   fase   _____

18. digit   dijit   _____

19. large   larj   _____

20. jem   gem   _____

Name _____   Date _____

Adjectives

Focus

- An **adjective** is a word that describes a noun. An adjective tells *how much*, *how many*, or *what kind*.

Example

There are **five** classes of **living** things.

- Articles are special kinds of adjectives. There are three articles: *a*, *an*, and *the*.

Example

An insect or **a** bird might be included in **the** animal class.

Practice   **Read the poem below. Circle the adjectives and articles.**

For a big green plant

Or a tiny little ant

Resting in the woods is nice.

Each living thing must

Share cool shade and just

Take a break in paradise.

Circle the adjectives and underline the articles in the sentences below.

1. A duck likes to spend time in the water.

2. Clumsy swans find it hard to walk on the ground.

3. Raptors have pointed beaks to tear things.

4. A penguin uses its wings to swim in the ocean.

5. Large ostriches can be as big as eight feet tall.

Read the paragraph below. Underline the articles and circle the adjectives.

Many creatures live in the forest. Blue

peacocks and brown owls live in the forests. Red

deer and gray squirrels live there, too. Green frogs

live in the forests that are near water. Sometimes,

a white rabbit can be found hopping through the

forest. How many bears have you seen in the

forest? I saw two bears last year.

Name _____ Date _____

/s/ Sound and Spellings

Focus • The /s/ sound can be spelled *ce*, *ci_*, and *cy*.

Practice Read each word aloud. Underline the spelling pattern that makes the /s/ sound.

1. ice

2. policy

3. pencil

4. center

5. lacy

6. city

7. trace

8. civil

Use the words in the box to complete each sentence.

rice	circle	fancy	juicy	circus

1. Draw a square, triangle, and _____.

2. Patsy has a _____ dress.

3. The watermelon was very _____.

4. May I please have more _____?

5. We went to the _____.

UNIT 2 **Lesson 5**

Apply   Choose a word from the box that makes sense in the sentence. Write the word on the line.

1. We went out to eat dinner.

The pizza was in the shape of a

large _____.

I ate three _____.

| circle |
| fancy |
| slices |

2. My sister loves going to school.

_____ is in the ninth grade.

Her favorite subject is _____.

| space |
| science |
| Nancy |

3. Rebecca enjoys spending time with her family.

She lives in the same _____
as her brother.

Rebecca's _____ likes to play with her.

| niece |
| city |
| race |

4. Ned goes to see a movie every Saturday.

A fancy name for a movie is _____.

Today's movie is about two funny _____.

| circus |
| mice |
| cinema |

Phonics • *Skills Practice 1*

Name _____ **Date** _____

/j/ Sound and Spellings

Focus • The /j/ sound can be spelled *ge* and *gi*.

Practice Read each word aloud. Underline the spelling pattern that makes the /j/ sound.

1. rage   **5.** cringe

2. logic   **6.** giraffe

3. giant   **7.** orange

4. gentle   **8.** fragile

Draw a line connecting one word on the left with a rhyming word on the right.

1. budge   **a.** magic

2. cage   **b.** fudge

3. twinge   **c.** frigid

4. tragic   **d.** page

5. rigid   **e.** hinge

Apply Look at the pairs of words below. Choose the word that best completes the sentence and write the word on the line.

1. Angela left a _____ for you.
   (message, messagi)

2. The car's _____ is making funny sounds.
   (engene, engine)

3. 153 is a three-_____ number.
   (digit, diget)

4. Use your _____ to write a story.
   (imagenation, imagination)

5. My aunt lives in a tiny _____.
   (cottage, cottagi)

6. Park the car in our _____.
   (garagi, garage)

7. The glass vase is very _____.
   (fragele, fragile)

8. Did you hear that _____ sound?
   (strange, stangi)

9. I would like a _____ drink, please.
   (lagi, large)

10. We will pay for our things at the cash _____.
    (register, regester)

Name _____ Date _____

Selection Vocabulary

Focus

trunks *n.* Plural of **trunk**: the main part of a tree where the branches grow out.

sprouts *v.* Begins to grow.

limbs *n.* Plural of **limb**: a branch of a tree.

minerals *n.* Plural of **mineral**: something found underground and used as food for plants growing in soil.

stems *n.* Plural of **stem**: the main part of a plant.

Practice Circle *Yes* or *No* if the boldfaced definition of the underlined word in each sentence makes sense.

1. Initials were carved in the tree's <u>trunk</u>.
   main part of a tree where the branches grow out .... Yes   No

2. A plant <u>sprouts</u> from a tiny seed.
   begins to grow .... Yes   No

3. Cut the <u>stems</u> of the flowers.
   a branch of a tree .... Yes   No

4. Roots of a tree get <u>minerals</u> from the soil.
   begins to grow .... Yes   No

5. Don't hang from that tree <u>limb</u>!
   a branch of a tree .... Yes   No

Apply Write the vocabulary word from the word box to complete each sentence.

| trunk | limbs | stem | sprouts | minerals |

1. Plants get the _____ they need from the soil.

2. A hard, woody stem of a tree is called its

_____.

3. Trees _____ from the ground as they begin to grow.

4. Along with the trunk, _____ are part of a tree's stem.

5. The _____ is the main part of any plant.

Answer the following questions.

What is the name of the hard layer of wood that covers a tree

trunk? _____

What are the two parts of a tree's *stem*?

_____

Selection Vocabulary • *Skills Practice 1*

Name _____ Date _____

Classify and Categorize

Focus
- **Classifying** and **categorizing** means putting things into groups.
- Readers sort information into different groups or **categories**.
- **Classifying** can help readers keep track of information in the story. To classify information:
  - name the categories for things, characters, or events
  - list the things, characters, or events that fit under each category
  - sometimes things, characters, or events can fit into more than one category

Practice Make a list for each category below.

Things I like to do

1. _____
2. _____
3. _____
4. _____

Things I don't like to do

1. _____
2. _____
3. _____
4. _____

Apply **Read the following paragraph.**

Tree leaves can come in many shapes and sizes. However, there are only two different groups of trees. One group is evergreen and the other group is broadleaf. Most evergreen trees have needles that are thin and scale-like. Some examples of evergreen trees are spruce, cypress, pine, and hemlock. Broadleaf trees have flatter, wider leaves. Beech, maple, oak, and hickory are types of broadleaf trees.

Use the chart below to classify and categorize the information in the paragraph.

Types of Trees

Category: _____	Category: _____
1. _____	1. _____
2. _____	2. _____
3. _____	3. _____
4. _____	4. _____

Name _____ Date _____

Writing an Informative Report

Think | **Audience: Who** will read your informative report?

_____

Purpose: What is your reason for writing an informative report?

_____

Prewriting | **Plan your report by choosing your topic and asking three questions about your topic. Then write the facts in the web below.**

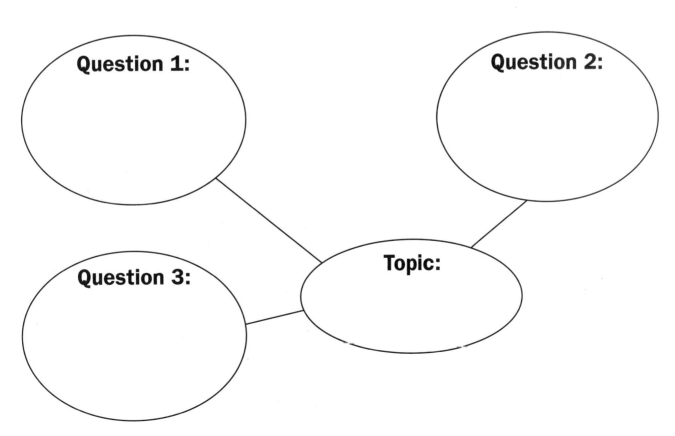

Question 1:

Question 2:

Question 3:

Topic:

Revising   Use this checklist to revise.

☐ Did you answer all of your questions?

☐ Do you have one paragraph for each question?

☐ Did you use facts and special words correctly?

☐ Do your ideas and information flow smoothly from one sentence to another?

☐ Is your report written in an interesting, lively way?

Editing/Proofreading   Use this checklist to correct mistakes.

☐ Is every paragraph indented?

☐ Is every word or special term spelled correctly?

☐ Did you capitalize people's names and place names?

☐ Does every sentence start with a capital letter?

☐ Does every sentence end with correct punctuation?

Publishing   Use this checklist to prepare for publication.

☐ Write or type a neat copy of your report.

☐ Include a drawing, photograph, or other visual aid to go with your report.

☐ Read your report aloud to the whole class or small groups of classmates.

Name _____ **Date** _____

Long e spelled _ie_, _y, ee, ea, e, and e_e
/s/ spelled ce and ci_
/j/ spelled ge and gi_

Focus
- Long vowels sound like their name.
- The long e sound can be spelled _ie_, _y, ee, ea, e, and e_e.
- The /s/ sound can be spelled ce and ci_.
- The /j/ sound can be spelled ge and gi_.

Word List
1. very
2. germ
3. cell
4. civil
5. chief
6. funny
7. field
8. rigid
9. baby
10. brief

Challenge Words
11. grieve
12. cancel

Practice Sort the spelling words under the correct heading.

Long e spelled _ie_

1. _____
2. _____
3. _____

Long e spelled _y

4. _____
5. _____
6. _____

/j/ spelled ge

7. _____

/j/ spelled gi_

8. _____

/s/ spelled ce

9. _____

/s/ spelled ci_

10. _____

Apply Meaning Strategy

very	chief	circle	funny	baby

Fill in the blank with a spelling word from the box.

11. _____ the words from your spelling list.

12. The police _____ helped train the new recruits.

13. The new puppy looked _____ trying to walk on its hind legs.

14. It was _____ hot outside today.

15. The _____ is ready for his bottle.

Visualization Strategy Circle the correct spelling for each word. Write the correctly spelled word on the line.

18. jurm   germ   _____

19. brief   breef   _____

20. field   feeld   _____

21. celle   cell   _____

22. rigid   rijud   _____

Name _____   Date _____ __

Singular and Plural Nouns

Focus
- Nouns can be **singular** or **plural**.
- A **singular noun** names one.

Example
  star   animal   plant   idea

- **Plural nouns** name more than one.

Example
  star**s**   animal**s**   plant**s**   idea**s**

- Most nouns add **–s** to form the plural form.

Example
  car**s**   bike**s**   train**s**

- Some nouns add **–es** to words ending in *s, x, z, ss, ch,* or *sh*.

Example
  brush   brush**es**
  box   box**es**

- Other nouns ending in *y* change the *y* to *i* and add –es.

Example
  buddy   budd**ies**

- There are some special nouns. These nouns change when they are made plural.

Example
  person   people

Practice Circle the plural nouns and underline the singular nouns in the sentences below.

1. There is an imaginary line around the middle of our planet.

2. This line is called the equator.

3. The equator divides the earth into two hemispheres.

4. Some parts of the world are always hot.

5. At the equator, climates are hot and rainy.

Apply Write the plural form of each noun below.

1. ax _____

2. rocket _____

3. hat _____

4. man _____

5. sky _____

6. wish _____

Name _____ Date _____

/ī/ Sound and Spellings

Focus • The /ī/ sound can be spelled _igh, _y, and _ie.

Practice Underline the spelling pattern for the /ī/ sound in each of the following words.

1. tight

2. my

3. lie

4. why

5. slight

6. spies

7. style

8. light

Change the first letter to make a new rhyming word. Write the word on the line.

1. high _____

2. cry _____

3. tie _____

4. fight _____

5. why _____

6. fried _____

Apply   **Choose a word from the word box to complete each sentence.**

tight	quiet	shy	bright	rhyme	fried

1. Please be very _____ in the hallway.

2. She used a _____ yellow crayon.

3. Do the words 'night' and 'might' _____?

4. The new student seemed to be _____.

5. Peter's shirt was too _____.

6. Angie made _____ chicken for lunch.

Add one of the following letters to the words below. Use each letter one time.

c	n	l	b	s	p

1. ____ight   **4.** ____ight

2. ____y   **5.** ____ie

3. ____ie   **6.** ____ry

Name _____ **Date** _____

/ī/ Sound and Spellings

Focus • The /ī/ sound can be spelled *i* and *i_e*.

Practice Unscramble the following words. Write the word on the line and the spelling pattern that makes the /ī/ sound.

1. i d y t _____ _____

2. p i e p _____ _____

3. k n d i _____ _____

4. m t e i _____ _____

5. c d i e _____ _____

Write a sentence with each word from above.

1. _____

2. _____

3. _____

4. _____

5. _____

UNIT 3 **Lesson 1**

Apply Choose a word from the word box to complete each sentence.

behind	bite	wide	idea	climb	pile

1. May I have a _____ of your dessert?

2. Owen had an _____ of a game to play.

3. Let's _____ up the ladder!

4. We all jumped in the _____ of leaves.

5. The opposite of narrow is _____.

6. What is _____ the curtain?

Draw a line matching a word on the left to the rhyming word on the right.

1. spiny   **a.** kite

2. find   **b.** dime

3. white   **c.** tiny

4. lime   **d.** mind

Name _____ Date _____

Selection Vocabulary

Focus

public *adj.* For all the people.

automatically *v.* Working by itself.

recognize *v.* To know and remember from before.

perched *v.* Past tense of **perch**: to stand, sit, or rest on a raised place.

practice *v.* To do something over and over to gain skill.

Practice   **Write the vocabulary word that matches each definition below.**

1. _____ to stand, sit, or rest on a raised place

2. _____ to do something over and over to gain skill

3. _____ working by itself

4. _____ for all the people

5. _____ to know and remember from before

Apply Circle the correct word that completes the sentence.

1. A bird was _____ on top of the tree.
   a. practice   **b.** perched

2. Did you _____ Mr. Williams?
   a. recognize   **b.** public

3. The traffic light _____ changes colors.
   a. recognize   **b.** automatically

4. Is the park open to the _____?
   a. public   **b.** perched

5. Henry will _____ throwing a ball.
   a. practice   **b.** recognize

Write the vocabulary word you think of after reading each word.

public	recognize	practice	automatically	perch

1. sit _____   **4.** itself _____

2. skill _____   **5.** remember _____

3. people _____

Name _____ **Date** _____

Timed Writing

Think

Audience: Who will read your paragraph?

_____

Purpose: What do you want your paragraph to do?

_____

Timed Writing Strategies

1. Read the entire prompt.

2. Circle the directions for writing the paper.

3. Underline each thing you are asked to write about.

4. Read through each reminder.

5. Take a few minutes to make notes about your subject.

Revising Use this checklist to revise.

☐ Does each sentence help the reader understand your writing?

☐ Did you use specific details?

☐ Are your details organized and in order?

☐ Did you respond to each reminder in the writing prompt?

Editing/Proofreading Use this checklist to correct mistakes.

☐ Is your paragraph indented?

☐ Did you use complete sentences?

☐ Is every word or special term spelled correctly?

☐ Does every sentence start with a capital letter?

☐ Does every sentence end with correct punctuation?

Name _____ Date _____

Long i spelled _igh, _y, _ie, i, and i_e

Focus
- Long vowels sound like their names.
- The long i sound can be spelled _igh, _y, _ie, i, and i_e.

Practice Sort the spelling words under the correct heading.

long i spelled _igh

1. _____
2. _____

long i spelled _y

3. _____
4. _____
5. _____

long i spelled _ie

6. _____
7. _____

long i spelled i

8. _____

long i spelled i_e

9. _____
10. _____

Word List

1. pie
2. night
3. fly
4. pile
5. child
6. right
7. shy
8. lie
9. mice
10. try

Challenge Words

11. recognize
12. skyscraper
13. style
14. knight
15. mighty

Apply Rhyming Strategy Write the spelling word or words that rhyme with each set of words below. The new word will have the same spelling pattern for the long i sound. The first one is done for you.

16. tie   die   pie   lie

17. cry   dry   _____ _____ _____

18. dice   twice   _____

19. flight   might   _____ _____

20. file   mile   _____

Visualization Strategy Circle the correct spelling for each word. Write the correct spelling on the line.

21. nyte   night   _____

22. child   chield   _____

23. mighce   mice   _____

24. pie   py   _____

25. try   trie   _____

Name _____ Date _____

Comparative Adjectives

Focus
- An **adjective** describes a noun or pronoun. You can use **comparative adjectives** to compare nouns or pronouns.

- Most adjectives that compare two nouns or pronouns end in **–er**.

- Most adjectives that compare more than two nouns or pronouns end in **–est**.

- Some adjectives use **more** and **most**. Use **more** to compare two things. Use **most** to compare more than two things.

Practice Circle the comparative adjective in each sentence below. Underline the nouns being compared.

1. Henry is taller than John.

2. The parrot is more colorful than the robin.

Apply Circle the correct word to complete each sentence.

1. You are the _____ girl I know!

        luckier   luckiest

2. Peacocks have the _____ beautiful feathers.

        more   most

Articles

• An **adjective** describes a noun or pronoun.
Articles are special kinds of adjectives.

• The three articles are: *a*, *an*, and *the*.

Practice   Circle the article in each sentence.
Underline the noun it describes.

1. The play is tomorrow.

2. She found a dress in her mom's closet.

3. She added an apron to the dress.

Apply   Write the correct article on the blank line to
complete each sentence.

a	an	the

1. Did you find _____ coat to wear?

2. _____ octopus has eight legs.

3. Mrs. Jones is _____ principal.

Name _____ Date _____

/ō/ Sound and Spellings

Focus • The /ō/ sound can be spelled _ow, and oa_.

Practice Use the 'equations' to add (+) and remove (-) letters to create different *ow* and *oa* words.

1. glow – g + f = _____ – f + b = _____

2. grow – g + c = _____ – c + th = _____

3. coat – c + b = _____ – b + m = _____

4. road – r + t = _____ – t + l = _____

Write a sentence using one word from each equation above. Circle the spelling pattern in the word you chose for each sentence.

1. _____

2. _____

3. _____

4. _____

Apply Read the word in the box. Then read the sentence. Change the word in the box to make a new rhyming word to complete the sentence.

1. | **tow** | Did you _____ the lawn today?

2. | **hollow** | Did you _____ my directions?

3. | **coal** | Did you see me score a soccer _____?

4. | **willow** | Did you use my _____ last night?

5. | **roast** | Did you want _____ with your eggs?

6. | **moan** | Did the bank _____ you some money?

7. | **fellow** | Did you color the picture of a sun _____?

8. | **row** | Did you tie the ribbon into a _____?

9. | **grow** | Did you see the black _____ fly away?

10. | **throat** | Did you watch the boat _____ on the water?

Name _____ Date _____

/ō/ Sound and Spellings

Focus • The /ō/ sound can be spelled o, and o_e.

Practice Use the letters in parentheses ( ) to add to the given spelling pattern to make a word. The letters in parentheses ( ) do not have to go in the order that they are written. Write the new word on the line.

1. (s, m, t)   __ o __ __   _____

2. (v, t)   __ o __ e   _____

3. (s, t, p)   __ o __ __   _____

4. (c, k, h, e)   __ __ o __ e   _____

Change the word in the box to make a new rhyming word that will complete the sentence.

1. | mow | The car broke down so we had to call a

_____ truck.

2. | oats | We hang our _____ on the hooks on the wall.

3. | note | Ally _____ a letter to her Uncle Joe.

Apply   Choose a word from the box to complete each sentence.

motion	solo	close	whole	over
oval	soda	slope	frozen	those

1. Mariah is going to sing a _____ at the concert.

2. Would you like a glass of milk instead of _____ to drink?

3. We have to clean up this _____ mess quickly!

4. John can draw a circle, square, triangle, and

_____.

5. Peter forgot to _____ the door.

6. We can ice skate on the _____ lake.

7. Do _____ shoes belong to you?

8. Let's ski down the bunny _____.

9. Is the movie _____ already?

10. The _____ of the boat made me seasick.

Name _____ Date _____

Selection Vocabulary

Focus

employees *n.* Plural of **employee**: a person who works for a person or business for pay.

borrow *v.* To receive something with the understanding that it must be given back.

deposits *n.* Plural of **deposit**: money added to a bank account.

vault *n.* A room or compartment that is used to store money or other things of value.

withdrawals *n.* Plural of **withdrawal**: money taken out of a bank account.

Practice **Write the vocabulary word that will complete each sentence.**

1. There are many _____ working at the bank.

2. People _____ money from the bank to buy big items.

3. _____ are made when you add money to your account.

4. When you take money out of your account, it is a

   _____ .

5. The _____ is a safe place to store important things.

Apply Use your knowledge of the vocabulary words from this lesson to complete the following activities.

1. Write two examples of jobs done by bank *employees*.

_____

_____

2. What is something you may buy that you would need to *borrow* money from the bank to purchase?

_____

3. These are your *deposits*: $10.00, $10.00, and $5.00. How much money do you have in your bank account?

_____

4. Now, if you *withdraw* $5.00, how much money is left in your bank account?

_____

5. Write an item that you might keep in a bank vault.

_____

Selection Vocabulary • *Skills Practice 1*

Name _____ Date _____

Timed Writing

Think **Audience: Who** will read your paragraph?

_____

Purpose: What do you want your paragraph to do?

_____

Timed Writing Strategies

1. Read the entire prompt.

2. Circle the directions for writing the paper.

3. Underline each thing you are asked to write about.

4. Read through each reminder.

5. Take a few minutes to make notes about your subject.

Revising Use this checklist to revise.

☐ Does each sentence help the reader understand your writing?

☐ Did you use specific details?

☐ Are your details organized and in order?

☐ Did you respond to each reminder in the writing prompt?

Editing/Proofreading Use this checklist to correct mistakes.

☐ Is your paragraph indented?

☐ Did you use complete sentences?

☐ Is every word or special term spelled correctly?

☐ Does every sentence start with a capital letter?

☐ Does every sentence end with correct punctuation?

Name _____ **Date** _____

Long o spelled _ow, oa_, o, and o_e

Focus
- Long vowels sound like their names.
- The long o sound can be spelled _ow, oa_, o, and o_e.

Practice **Sort the spelling words under the correct heading.**

long o spelled _ow   long o spelled o

1. _____   9. _____

2. _____   long o spelled o_e

3. _____   10. _____

4. _____

long o spelled oa_

5. _____

6. _____

7. _____

8. _____

Word List
1. store
2. loan
3. grow
4. boat
5. know
6. toad
7. blow
8. coat
9. hello
10. show

Challenge Words
11. borrow
12. coast
13. below
14. robot
15. owe

Apply Consonant-Substitution Strategy Replace the underlined letter or letters to create a spelling word. The new word will have the same spelling for the long o sound.

16. <u>sh</u>ore + st = _____

17. <u>r</u>oad + t = _____

18. groan + l = _____

19. coa<u>l</u> + t = _____

20. goat + b = _____

| grow | boat | know | blow | show |

Meaning Strategy Write the correct spelling word on the line.

21. Do you _____ the answer to number 5?

22. I had to _____ up ten balloons for the party.

23. The _____ ride made me feel a little sick.

24. My favorite television _____ is on tonight.

25. Eating fruits and vegetables will help you _____ strong and healthy.

Name _____ Date _____

Capitalization: Days, Months, Cities, and States

Focus
- Calendars will help you remember to capitalize the **days** of the week and **months** of the year.
- You must also capitalize names of **cities** and **states**.

Practice **Write the name of the day or the month in each sentence below.**

1. The day before Wednesday is _____.

2. New Year's Day is the first of _____.

3. The last day of the year is in _____.

4. The day before Friday is _____.

5. Valentine's Day is in _____.

6. The day after Friday is _____.

Apply **Read the poem. Underline three times each letter that should be capitalized.**

Thirty days has september,

april, june, and november;

All the rest have thirty-one.

february has twenty-eight alone;

Save in leap year, at which time,

february's days are twenty-nine.

Read the paragraph. Underline three times each letter that should be capitalized.

My class was studying unusual names of cities in the

United States. I began my report on february 28, 2006. I

read about boulder, colorado. I wonder if the rocks in that

city are bigger than the rocks in little rock, arkansas. Do

buffaloes really live in buffalo, new york? Does everyone

sew in needles, california? I finished my report on

march 6, 3006.

Name _____ Date _____

/ī/ Sound and Spellings

Focus • The /ī/ sound can be spelled _igh, _y, and _ie.

Practice Write the correct spelling of each misspelled word.

1. nyte _____

2. trighed _____

3. drie _____

4. quyet _____

5. liet _____

6. shigh _____

Apply Choose a word from above to complete the sentence.

1. Lenny _____ his best.

2. Shh! Please be _____.

3. I went shopping last _____.

Focus   • The /ī/ sound can be spelled *i* and *i_e*.

Practice   **Choose a letter below to fill in the beginning blank of the words below. Write the word on the line.**

i	t	s	l

1. _____ire   _____

2. _____dol   _____

3. _____iar   _____

4. _____ize   _____

Apply   **Choose a word from the box that makes sense in the sentence. Write the word on the line.**

1. What can you do on a windy day?

Try flying a _____.

It will look like a _____ dot in the sky.

kite
tiny
sky

Name _____ Date _____

/ō/ Sound and Spellings

Focus
• The /ō/ sound can be spelled _ow, and oa_.

Practice Use the letters in parentheses ( ) to add to the spelling pattern given. Write the new word on the line. Letters in parentheses ( ) do not have to go in the order they are written.

1. (c, k, r) __ __ **o a** __ _____

2. (l, e, b) __ __ __ **o w** _____

3. (s, a, w, l, l) __ __ __ __ __ **o w** _____

4. (t, r, h, t) __ __ __ **o a** __ _____

5. (w, n, d, i) __ __ __ __ **o w** _____

Apply Write a sentence with each word from above.

1. _____

2. _____

3. _____

4. _____

5. _____

Skills Practice 1 • Phonics

/ō/ Sound and Spellings

Focus • The /ō/ sound can be spelled o and o_e.

Practice Circle the correct spelling for each word.

1. cocoa   coecoe

2. proetect   protect

3. hop   hope

4. cold   coeld

5. smoke   smok

Apply Use the correct spelling of each word above in a sentence.

1. _____

2. _____

3. _____

4. _____

5. _____

Name _____ Date _____

Selection Vocabulary

Focus

ingredients *n.* Plural of **ingredient**: a part that goes into a mixture.

culture *n.* The customs and beliefs of a group of people.

dough *n.* A mixture of flour, liquid, and other things that is usually baked.

jalapeño *n.* A small, hot pepper.

international *adj.* Having to do with two or more nations.

Practice   Complete the crossword puzzle.

Across

1. Having to do with two or more nations

4. The customs and beliefs of a group of people

5. A small hot pepper

Down

2. Parts that go in a mixture

3. A mixture of flour, liquid, and other things that is usually baked

Apply Use your knowledge of the vocabulary words to complete the following activities.

1. Write an example of a food that is made from *dough*.

_____

2. Write another word that could be used in place of the word *jalapeño*.

_____

3. Write one example of a custom from your family's *culture*.

_____

Write a sentence with each vocabulary word.

ingredients	dough	international	culture	jalapeño

1. _____

2. _____

3. _____

4. _____

5. _____

Name _____ **Date** _____

Fact and Opinion

Focus
- A **fact** is a statement that can be proven true.
- An **opinion** is what someone feels or believes is true. Opinions cannot be proven true or false.

Practice **Look at the statements from "Jalapeño Bagels". In the spaces next to each statement, write _fact_ if the statement is a fact. Write _opinion_ if the statement is an opinion.**

1. Jam is better than lox. _____

2. Chocolate bars are my favorite dessert. _____

3. Pan dulce is a Mexican sweet bread. _____

4. My father uses my grandmother's recipe to make the bagels.

   _____

5. The Jewish braided bread is too beautiful to eat.

   _____

6. My teacher told us to bring something to school from our

   culture. _____

Apply Add a fact and an opinion to each sentence below. Use the clues in parentheses ( ).

1. (opinion) Babies like to _____.

(fact) Babies drink _____.

2. (opinion) Globes are _____.

(fact) A globe shows _____.

Think about the story "Jalapeño Bagels". Write one sentence about food that is a fact and one that is an opinion.

Opinion:

3. _____

_____

Fact:

4. _____

_____

Name _____ Date _____

Explaining A Process

Think **Audience: Who** will read your paragraph?

_____

Purpose: What do you want your paragraph to do?

_____

Prewriting Use the space below to plan a paragraph that gives directions for a recipe. Remember to put your steps in order.

Recipe for: _____

First

_____

_____

_____

Then

_____

_____

_____

Second

_____

_____

_____

Finally

_____

_____

_____

Revising   Use this checklist to revise.

☐ Do your sentences describe steps in the correct order?

☐ Did you use time and order words to sequence the steps?

☐ Are there details that need to be added to make the directions clear?

☐ Will your reader be able to follow the directions easily?

Editing/Proofreading   Use this checklist to correct mistakes.

☐ Is your paragraph indented?

☐ Is every word or special term spelled correctly?

☐ Does every sentence start with a capital letter?

☐ Does every sentence end with correct punctuation?

Publishing   Use this checklist to prepare for publication.

☐ Write or type a neat copy.

☐ Include a drawing or a map that shows the steps in the right order.

☐ Ask someone if they can follow your directions.

Name _____ Date _____

Review: Long i and Long o Spellings

Focus
- Long vowels sound like their names.
- Long i can be spelled _igh, _y, _ie, i, and i_e.
- Long o can be spelled _ow, oa_, o, and o_e.

Practice Sort the spelling words under the correct heading.

long i spelled _igh

1. _____

long i spelled _ie

2. _____

long i spelled _y

3. _____

4. _____

long i spelled i_e

5. _____

long o spelled _ow

6. _____

7. _____

long o spelled oa_

8. _____

9. _____

long o spelled o_e

10. _____

Word List
1. dry
2. tie
3. fight
4. why
5. tow
6. soap
7. below
8. bike
9. cone
10. oak

Challenge Words
11. July
12. twilight
13. shallow
14. cocoa
15. thigh

Apply **Rhyming Strategy** **Find the spelling word that rhymes with each pair of words below. The correct word will have the same spelling pattern as the pair of words.**

17. bow   low   _____

18. hike   strike   _____

19. croak   soak   _____

20. light   night   _____

21. zone   phone   _____

Visualization Strategy **Circle the correct spelling for each spelling word. Write the correct spelling on the line.**

22. dry   drie   _____

23. bealoa   below   _____

24. why   wie   _____

25. tigh   tie   _____

26. soap   sope   _____

Name _____ Date _____

Commas: Words in a Series

 **Focus** • A **comma** is used after each item in a series or list of things except for the last one.

 **Practice** **Commas have been left out in the sentences below. Put commas where they are needed in the lists.**

1. Fleas flies and bees drive me crazy!

2. Insects eat things such as wood paper and even other insects.

3. Bats birds and reptiles also eat insects.

4. What is red juicy and healthy? An apple!

Find each sentence that has commas in the right place. Circle the letter in front of it.

1. a. Cars can be red, blue, black, or green.

  b. Trees can be tall short, thin or wide.

2. a. The American flag is red, white, and blue.

  b. The Italian flag is red white, and green.

Apply   **Write a list of items for each topic.**

Favorite Foods	**Favorite Animals**
1. _____	1. _____
2. _____	2. _____
3. _____	3. _____

Write a sentence for each topic, writing your list as a series of items using commas correctly.

1. _____

   _____

2. _____

   _____

Read the story and add commas where they are needed.
Use proofreading marks.

    Flowers have soft petals pretty colors and a nice smell. To grow flowers you must plant the seeds water the plants and pull the weeds. Flowers look pretty in a garden in your office or in your house. Today, we will plant purple pansies white daisies and lilies all around the border of the garden.

Name _____ **Date** _____

/ū/ Sound and Spellings

Focus • The /ū/ sound can be spelled _ew and _ue.

Practice Read the following words aloud.

cue	argue	nephew	fuel	review	pew

Write the words with the /ū/ sound spelled like _Sue_.

1. _____ 3. _____

2. _____

Write the words with the /ū/ sound spelled like _few_.

1. _____ 3. _____

2. _____

Underline the _ue or _ew spelling pattern. Change the first letter of the word to make a rhyming word with the same spelling pattern. Write the new word on the line.

1. hue _____ **2.** few _____

 Choose a word from the box to complete each sentence.

statue	barbecue	nephew	review	argue
few	value	view	curfew	rescue

1. Alice has a niece and a _____.

2. What will we eat at the _____?

3. There were only a _____ people at the store.

4. My sister and I sometimes _____ over toys.

5. The _____ of friendship is priceless.

6. What a beautiful _____ of the forest!

7. Mr. Williams will _____ the spelling words.

8. Stand as still as a _____.

9. A firefighter will _____ the kitten.

10. My _____ is nine o'clock tonight.

Phonics • *Skills Practice 1*

Name _____ **Date** _____

/ū/ Sound and Spellings

Focus • The /ū/ sound can be spelled u and u_e.

Practice Read the following words aloud.

humor	museum	cube	used	unit	amuse

Write the words with the /ū/ sound spelled like *human*.

1. _____ 3. _____

2. _____

Write the words with the /ū/ sound spelled like *huge*.

1. _____ 3. _____

2. _____

Use one word with the *u* spelling pattern and one word with the *u_e* spelling pattern from above to complete the sentence.

His sense of _____ did not _____ me.

Apply **Circle the word in the sentence with the /ū/ sound. Write the word and the spelling pattern used on the blank lines.**

1. Paula is allowed to play a game on the computer.

_____   _____

2. Adam refused to eat his broccoli.

_____   _____

3. I can see the birds better by looking through my binoculars.

_____   _____

4. The menu has a list of all the desserts.

_____   _____

5. We had a party to give tribute to our teacher.

_____   _____

Name _____ **Date** _____

Selection Vocabulary

Focus

taxes *n.* Plural of **tax**: money that people or businesses must pay to support the government.

council *n.* A group of people who make decisions for a larger group.

cashier *n.* A person in charge of paying out or receiving money.

elect *v.* To choose by voting.

routes *n.* Plural of **route**: a road or other course used for traveling.

mayor *n.* The person who is the head of a city or town government.

Practice **Draw a line to match each word on the left to its definition on the right.**

1. cashier

2. elect

3. taxes

4. mayor

5. routes

6. council

a. person who is head of a city or town government

b. road or other course used for traveling

c. to choose by voting

d. person in charge of paying or receiving money

e. money that people or businesses pay the government for its support

f. a group of people who make decisions for a larger group

1. Our class will <u>elect</u> a new student body president.
choose by voting...Yes   No

2. The <u>mayor</u> gave me a key to the city.
**person who is the head of a city or
town government** ....Yes   No

3. Mom paid the <u>cashier</u> for our groceries.
to choose by voting....................................Yes   No

4. The <u>council</u> made a decision.
**group of people who make decisions
for a larger group** ....Yes   No

5. Everyone must pay <u>taxes</u>.
a road or other course used for traveling..............Yes   No

6. Which <u>route</u> is the best way to get to school?
**a road or other course used
for traveling** ....Yes   No

Name _____ Date _____

Drawing Conclusions

Focus • Readers get ideas, or **draw conclusions**, about what is happening in a story by using clues from the story.

Practice **Read the sentences below. Then use the clues to draw a conclusion.**

- The classes at the town's dance school are always full.

- Many people watch when the dance students perform.

- Most children in town say they want to study dance.

- The dance school is moving to a bigger building next year.

Conclusion: _____

- Tom buys food at the pet store once a week.

- The many cages need to be cleaned daily.

- He enjoys spending time playing with his animal friends.

- Tom always says, "The more the merrier!"

Conclusion: _____

Apply   Write three sentences that are clues for the following conclusion.

Conclusion: It is raining outside.

1. _____

2. _____

3. _____

Now, write your own conclusion sentence and three sentences that will give clues.

Conclusion: _____

1. _____

2. _____

3. _____

Find a partner. Read the clues to your partner and write down their conclusion.

Partner's Conclusion: _____

Ask your partner which clue helped them the most. Write the clue below.

_____

Name _____ Date _____

Writing a Summary

Think   Audience: **Who** will read your summary?

_____

Purpose: **What** is your reason for writing your summary?

_____

Prewriting   **Use the graphic organizer below to write notes for your summary.**

Title of Article: _____

Main Idea: _____

_____

Detail about the main idea: _____

_____

Detail about the main idea: _____

_____

Detail about the main idea: _____

_____

Revising Use this checklist to revise.

☐ Did you choose an article related to the Unit theme?

☐ Did you tell the most important points of the article?

☐ Did you use your own words?

☐ Is there information that is not from the article?

☐ Will the reader understand the information?

Editing/Proofreading Use this checklist to correct mistakes.

☐ Make sure all of your sentences are complete.

☐ Is every word or special term spelled correctly?

☐ Does every sentence start with a capital letter and end with correct punctuation?

Publishing Use this checklist to prepare for publication.

☐ Write or type a neat copy.

☐ Attach the article you summarized.

Name _____ Date _____

Long u spelled _ew, _ue, u, and u_e

Focus

- Long vowels sound like their names.
- Some ways long u can be spelled are _ew, _ue, u, and u_e.

Practice Sort the spelling words under the correct heading.

long u spelled _ew   long u spelled u

1. _____   7. _____

2. _____   8. _____

long u spelled _ue   long u spelled u_e

3. _____   9. _____

4. _____   10. _____

5. _____

6. _____

Word List

1. cue
2. hue
3. few
4. music
5. pure
6. value
7. mew
8. cute
9. human
10. rescue

Challenge Words

11. fury
12. confuse
13. view
14. skew
15. argue

Apply Visualization Strategy Circle the correct spelling for each spelling word. Write the correct spelling on the line.

16. myoosic   music   _____

17. cute   kute   _____

18. reskew   rescue   _____

19. cue   kew   _____

20. mew   mue   _____

Proofreading Strategy Circle the misspelled words. Write the words correctly on the lines below.

Every yoomun has a special valew. However, very fyoo are quite as special as my Grandpa. His smile is like pewr sunshine. It brings a bright, golden hyue to the entire room. When I feel gloomy, it is so nice to have my Grandpa around to cheer me up!

21. _____

22. _____

23. _____

24. _____

25. _____

Name _____ Date _____

Subject/Verb Agreement

Focus
- A sentence has a **subject** and a **verb** that *agree*. This means that the subject and verb must both be singular, or they must both be plural.
- If the subject of a sentence is singular, the verb must be singular.
- If the subject of a sentence is plural, the verb must be plural.

Practice **Write *S* if the sentence has a singular subject and verb. Write *P* if the sentence has a plural subject and verb.**

1. Many plants can be kept inside to grow. _____

2. Herbs are plants used in cooking. _____

3. A wildflower grows by itself outside. _____

4. An evergreen tree keeps its leaves all year long. _____

Apply | Write *am*, *is*, or *are* to agree with the subject in each sentence.

1. We _____ learning about plants and trees.

2. A tree _____ a wooded plant.

3. I _____ enjoying these lessons.

Write *have* or *has* to agree with the subject in each sentence.

1. Evergreens _____ leaves or needles.

2. The desert _____ many plants.

Read the following sentences. Choose the verb in parentheses ( ) that correctly completes each sentence.

1. Bobby _____ the leaves in our yard when
       (rake, rakes)
it is autumn.

2. The leaves _____ from green to brown,
       (changes, change)
yellow, and orange.

3. We _____ a great time jumping in piles of leaves.
       (have, has)

Name _____ **Date** _____

Open and Closed Syllables

Focus
- An **open syllable** occurs when a syllable ends in a vowel. The vowel sound in an open syllable is usually long.

Example
di • ner   se • cret

- A **closed syllable** occurs when a vowel is followed by a consonant and the vowel usually has a short sound.

Example
win • ter   bet • ter

Practice Look at how the syllables are divided in the following words. Write open or closed to describe the syllables.

1. better   bet ter   _____

2. beside   be side   _____

3. faster   fast er   _____

4. rewind   re wind   _____

5. motion   mo tion   _____

Apply **Divide the following words into syllables. Then write open or closed to describe the syllables.**

1. closed _____   _____

2. running _____   _____

3. summer _____   _____

4. remote _____   _____

Write the following words under the heading of 'open' or 'closed' to describe the syllables.

winner	blanket	behind	token
paper	chosen	letter	forget

Open Syllables

1. _____

2. _____

3. _____

4. _____

Closed Syllables

1. _____

2. _____

3. _____

4. _____

Name _____ Date _____

/ū/ Sound and Spellings

Focus • The /ū/ sound can be spelled _ew and _ue.

Practice **Write *ew* or *ue* on the blank line to complete the word. Write the word.**

1. resc_____   _____

2. curf_____   _____

3. neph_____   _____

4. contin_____   _____

Apply **Use a word from above to complete each sentence.**

1. Did you _____ my toy from the trash can?

2. What time is your _____?

3. I am my uncle and aunt's _____.

4. Should we _____ reading the story?

Name _____ Date _____

/ū/ Sound and Spellings

Focus • The /ū/ sound can be spelled *u* and *u_e*.

Practice Add the letters in parentheses ( ) to the spelling pattern given to make a word. Write the word on the line. The letters in parentheses ( ) do not have to go in the order given.

1. (n, t, i)   **u** __ __ __   _____

2. (h ,d, m, i)   __ **u** __ __ __   _____

3. (t, c)   __ **u** __ **e**   _____

4. (f, s)   __ **u** __ **e**   _____

Apply   Use a word from above to complete each sentence.

1. It is a hot and _____ day outside.

2. My new puppy is so _____.

3. Did a _____ blow?

4. Our science _____ is about outer space.

Name _____ Date _____

Selection Vocabulary

Focus

aisles *n.* Plural of **aisle**: the space between two rows or sections of something.

sharp *adj.* Exact.

construction *v.* The act of building something.

arrangement *n.* A plan.

huddled *v.* Past tense of **huddle**: to crowd together.

tingle *v.* To have a slight stinging feeling.

Practice Write the vocabulary word that matches each definition below.

1. _____ a plan

2. _____ the act of building something

3. _____ exactly

4. _____ to crowd together

5. _____ to have a slight stinging feeling

6. _____ the space between two rows or sections of something

Apply   **Circle the correct word that completes the sentence.**

1. There were trucks and workers on the _____ site.
   a. construction   **b.** aisles   **c.** tingle

2. Different foods filled the _____ of the grocery store.
   a. sharp   **b.** aisles   **c.** arrangement

3. We _____ together to stay warm.
   a. aisles   **b.** sharp   **c.** huddled

4. Jessica and Abby have an _____ to share books.
   a. arrangement   **b.** huddled   **c.** tingle

5. Dinner will be at five o'clock _____!
   a. tingle   **b.** aisle   **c.** sharp

6. When I was sitting on the floor, my foot began to _____.
   a. huddled   **b.** tingle   **c.** sharp

Name _____ Date _____

Writing a Persuasive Paragraph

Think **Audience: Who** will read your persuasive paragraph?

_____

Purpose: What is your reason for writing a persuasive paragraph?

_____

Prewriting Use the graphic organizer to help you make your outline for a persuasive paragraph.

I. Topic: _____

   A. Main Heading: _____

   _____

     1. Supporting Reason: _____

     _____

     2. Supporting Reason: _____

     _____

     3. Supporting Reason: _____

     _____

Revising   Use this checklist to revise.

- ☐ Does your paragraph begin with a topic sentence?
- ☐ Is your purpose clear?
- ☐ Do you persuade others to think a certain way?
- ☐ Do you have good reasons that support your opinion?
- ☐ Are there facts or details that need to be added?

Editing/Proofreading   Use this checklist to correct mistakes.

- ☐ Is your paragraph indented?
- ☐ Is every word or special term spelled correctly?
- ☐ Does every sentence start with a capital letter?
- ☐ Does every sentence end with correct punctuation?

Publishing   Use this checklist to prepare for publication.

- ☐ Write or type a neat copy.
- ☐ Read your paragraph one more time. Make sure all the parts are there.
- ☐ Create a poster about your topic that will persuade others.

Name _____ Date _____

Open and Closed Syllables Review Long u

Focus
- Long vowels sound like their names.
- Long u can be spelled _ew, _ue, u, and u_e.
- Open syllables end in a vowel sound. The vowel sound is usually long.
- Closed syllables end in a vowel followed by a consonant. The vowel sound is usually short.

Word List
1. open
2. humid
3. until
4. person
5. cancel
6. fuel
7. begin
8. wagon
9. number
10. minus

Challenge Words
11. continue
12. dial
13. united
14. radio
15. moment

Practice Find the spelling words that have the long u sound.

1. _____ 2. _____

Find two spelling words that have open syllables.

3. _____ 4. _____

Find two spelling words that have closed syllables.

5. _____ 6. _____

UNIT 3 Lesson 5

Apply Proofreading Strategy Circle the spelling mistakes in the story below. Then write the misspelled words correctly on the lines.

Each pursin in our class will take a big math test today. We will begen at ten o'clock sharp. First, we will have to numbor our papers from one to ten. There will be questions like, "What is one hundred mynes thirty-nine?" and "What is six times seven?" Even though I studied hard, I am still nervous. I hope our teacher decides to kansul it!

7. _____   10. _____

8. _____   11. _____

9. _____

Meaning Strategy Write in words to complete the sentences below. Choose from the following words: open, humid, until, fuel, wagon.

12. I was sweating because it was so _____ outside.

13. You must remain seated _____ you finish your dinner.

14. In pioneer days, traveling by _____ was very common.

15. We need to _____ the window to let in some fresh air.

16. Let's make sure there is enough _____ in the car before we drive to Grandma's.

216 UNIT 3 • Lesson 5

Spelling • *Skills Practice 1*

Name _____ Date _____

Parts of a Book

Focus You can find all kinds of important information in books when you know where to look.

Practice Pick one of your textbooks and use what you have learned about the parts of a book to find the following information.

1. Title of book: _____

_____

2. Author: _____

_____

3. Copyright date: _____

_____

4. Does the table of contents show chapters, units, or story

titles? _____

_____

How many are there? _____

Write the name of one and the page on which it begins.

_____

_____

5. Does your book have a glossary? _____

_____

If yes, what is the first word listed? _____

_____

6. Does your book have an index? _____

_____

If yes, on what page does it begin? _____

_____

Name _____ **Date** _____

Contractions

- **Contractions** make writing sound more like a conversation. There are two kinds of contractions. A **contraction** can be formed by putting together a verb and the word *not*.

Examples

are not—aren't   do not—don't
did not—didn't   has not—hasn't
was not—wasn't   could not—couldn't

- A **contraction** may be formed by combining a pronoun and a verb.

Example
I am—I'm

Circle the correct contraction in each sentence below.

1. Greenland **isn't don't** a continent.

2. There **won't aren't** a lot of people living in Greenland.

3. Hawaii **wasn't weren't** a state until 1959.

Apply **Write the contraction for the boldfaced words in each sentence below.**

1. I am going to Arizona in April. _____

2. I have never been to the Southwest. _____

3. I will send you a postcard of the desert. _____

4. She is my best friend. _____

5. I know **he is** coming to visit today. _____

Add apostrophes where needed to make contractions. Use proofreading marks.

I couldnt think of anything to write. Were supposed to write a poem for class. It doesnt have to be a long poem. I cant think tonight! Couldnt I write about my life? I could, if it werent so late.

Write the contraction for the following words.

1. should not _____ **3.** have not _____

2. he is _____ **4.** there is _____

Name _____ **Date** _____

Proofreading Marks

¶   Indent

¶ Once upon a time, many years ago, there lived a dinosaur named Rocky. He lived . . .

∧   Add something.

a penny
shiny ∧

ℓ   Take out something.

Rabbits live in in burrows.

≡   Make a capital letter.

california
≡

/   Make a small letter.

We go camping in Summer.

sp⊘   Check spelling.

sp
(freind)

⊙   Add a period.

There are eight planets in the solar system ⊙